60 Potato Recipes for Home

By: Kelly Johnson

Table of Contents

Classic Potato Dishes:

- Perfect Roast Potatoes
- Mashed Potatoes with Garlic and Herbs
- Scalloped Potatoes
- Baked Potato Skins with Cheese and Bacon
- Hasselback Potatoes
- Potato Gnocchi with Sage Butter
- Loaded Potato Soup
- Potato Pancakes (Latkes)
- Potatoes Au Gratin
- Cheesy Twice-Baked Potatoes

International Flavors:

- Spanish Patatas Bravas
- Indian Aloo Gobi (Potato and Cauliflower)
- Irish Colcannon
- Greek Lemon Potatoes
- Japanese Sweet Potato Tempura
- French Gratin Dauphinois
- German Potato Salad
- Swedish Hasselback Sweet Potatoes
- Mexican Papas con Chorizo
- Italian Potato Gnocchi in Tomato Sauce

Healthy Potato Options:

- Baked Sweet Potato Fries
- Roasted Garlic Rosemary Sweet Potatoes
- Grilled Potato Skewers with Herbs
- Spiralized Potato Noodles with Pesto
- Sweet Potato and Black Bean Stuffed Peppers
- Crispy Oven-Baked Potato Wedges
- Greek Yogurt Potato Salad

- Sweet Potato and Quinoa Patties
- Spicy Roasted Potatoes
- Vegan Loaded Sweet Potato

Breakfast and Brunch:

- Potato and Spinach Breakfast Casserole
- Hash Browns with Bell Peppers and Onions
- Sweet Potato Hash with Poached Eggs
- Irish Boxty (Potato Pancakes)
- Breakfast Stuffed Potatoes
- Cheesy Potato and Bacon Breakfast Burritos
- Spanish Potato Omelette (Tortilla Española)
- Loaded Sweet Potato Breakfast Bowl
- Southwest Potato and Egg Skillet
- Potato and Chorizo Breakfast Tacos

Side Dishes and Salads:

- Warm Potato Salad with Mustard Vinaigrette
- Dill Pickle Potato Salad
- Lemon Herb Roasted Potato Salad
- Sweet Potato and Black Bean Salad
- Caprese Potato Salad
- Potato and Green Bean Salad
- Moroccan Spiced Roasted Potatoes
- Roasted Sweet Potato and Chickpea Salad
- Creamy Dijon Potato Salad
- Roasted Red Pepper and Potato Gratin

Creative Potato Recipes:

- Truffle Parmesan Potato Stacks
- Loaded Potato Pierogi
- Pesto Potato Pizzas
- Potato and Leek Soup
- Baked Potato Pizza with Bacon and Ranch
- Miso Glazed Sweet Potatoes
- Potato and Mushroom Tacos

- Greek Feta and Olive Stuffed Sweet Potatoes
- Cajun Spiced Potato Wedge Nachos
- Potato and Corn Chowder

Classic Potato Dishes:

Perfect Roast Potatoes

Ingredients:

- 4 large russet potatoes, peeled and cut into chunks
- 1/4 cup olive oil
- Salt and pepper, to taste
- 1 teaspoon garlic powder (optional)
- 1 teaspoon dried rosemary or thyme (optional)
- Chopped fresh parsley for garnish (optional)

Instructions:

Preheat the Oven:
- Preheat your oven to 425°F (220°C). Place a large baking sheet in the oven while it's preheating.

Prepare the Potatoes:
- Peel the potatoes and cut them into evenly sized chunks. Rinse the potatoes under cold water to remove excess starch.

Parboil the Potatoes:
- Place the potato chunks in a large pot of cold, salted water. Bring to a boil and let them simmer for about 8-10 minutes until the edges are just starting to soften. You don't want them fully cooked.

Drain and Dry:
- Drain the potatoes in a colander and let them sit for a few minutes to steam dry. You want the surface of the potatoes to be dry before roasting.

Coat with Olive Oil:
- In a bowl, toss the parboiled potatoes with olive oil until they are well-coated. You can add garlic powder, dried rosemary, or thyme for extra flavor if desired.

Season:
- Season the potatoes generously with salt and pepper. The preheated baking sheet will help create a crispy crust on the potatoes.

Roast in the Oven:
- Carefully transfer the potatoes onto the hot baking sheet in a single layer. Roast in the preheated oven for about 40-50 minutes, flipping them halfway through, or until the potatoes are golden brown and crispy.

Serve:
- Once the potatoes are done, remove them from the oven. Sprinkle with additional salt if needed and garnish with chopped fresh parsley if desired.

Enjoy:
- Serve the perfect roast potatoes as a delightful side dish to complement your main course.

These roast potatoes are crispy on the outside and fluffy on the inside, making them a delicious accompaniment to any meal. Feel free to customize the seasonings to suit your taste preferences.

Mashed Potatoes with Garlic and Herbs

Ingredients:

- 4 large potatoes (such as Russet), peeled and cut into chunks
- 4 cloves garlic, minced
- 1/2 cup unsalted butter
- 1/2 cup milk (whole milk or cream for a richer taste)
- Salt and pepper, to taste
- 2 tablespoons fresh parsley, finely chopped (optional)
- 1 teaspoon fresh thyme leaves, chopped (optional)
- Grated Parmesan cheese for garnish (optional)

Instructions:

Boil the Potatoes:
- Place the peeled and chopped potatoes in a large pot of salted water. Bring to a boil and simmer until the potatoes are fork-tender, usually about 15-20 minutes.

Drain the Potatoes:
- Drain the cooked potatoes in a colander.

Prepare Garlic Butter:
- While the potatoes are boiling, melt the butter in a small saucepan over medium heat. Add minced garlic and cook for 1-2 minutes until fragrant. Be careful not to brown the garlic.

Mash the Potatoes:
- Return the drained potatoes to the pot. Mash them using a potato masher or a fork until the desired consistency is reached.

Add Garlic Butter:
- Pour the garlic butter over the mashed potatoes.

Add Milk:
- Gradually add the milk while continuing to mash the potatoes. Adjust the amount of milk based on your desired creaminess.

Season:
- Season the mashed potatoes with salt and pepper to taste. Mix well.

Add Herbs:
- Stir in chopped fresh parsley and thyme for an extra burst of flavor. Reserve some for garnish if desired.

Garnish and Serve:
- Transfer the mashed potatoes to a serving dish. Garnish with additional herbs and a sprinkle of grated Parmesan cheese if desired.

Enjoy:
- Serve the garlic and herb mashed potatoes hot as a delicious side dish alongside your favorite main course.

These mashed potatoes are rich, creamy, and infused with the wonderful flavors of garlic and herbs. Feel free to customize the herbs to your liking and adjust the consistency with more or less milk as needed.

Scalloped Potatoes

Ingredients:

- 4 large potatoes, peeled and thinly sliced (about 1/8 inch thick)
- 1/4 cup unsalted butter
- 1/4 cup all-purpose flour
- 2 cups milk (whole milk or a combination of milk and cream for richness)
- 2 cloves garlic, minced
- 1 teaspoon salt
- 1/2 teaspoon black pepper
- 1/4 teaspoon ground nutmeg (optional)
- 1 1/2 cups shredded cheddar cheese
- Fresh thyme or parsley for garnish (optional)

Instructions:

Preheat the Oven:
- Preheat your oven to 350°F (175°C).

Prepare the Potatoes:
- Peel and thinly slice the potatoes. You can use a mandoline slicer for even slices.

Make the Sauce:
- In a medium saucepan, melt the butter over medium heat. Add minced garlic and cook for 1-2 minutes until fragrant.
- Stir in the flour to create a roux. Cook for another 2 minutes, stirring constantly.
- Gradually whisk in the milk, ensuring there are no lumps. Continue cooking and whisking until the sauce thickens, about 5-7 minutes.
- Season the sauce with salt, pepper, and nutmeg (if using). Remove from heat.

Layer the Potatoes:
- In a buttered baking dish, arrange a layer of sliced potatoes. Pour a portion of the sauce over the potatoes, then sprinkle a layer of shredded cheddar cheese. Repeat until all potatoes and sauce are used, finishing with a layer of cheese on top.

Bake:

- Cover the baking dish with aluminum foil and bake in the preheated oven for about 45 minutes. Then, uncover and bake for an additional 15-20 minutes or until the top is golden brown, and the potatoes are tender.

Garnish and Serve:
- Remove from the oven and let it rest for a few minutes. Garnish with fresh thyme or parsley if desired.

Enjoy:
- Serve the scalloped potatoes as a delicious side dish, perfect for holiday dinners or any special occasion.

These scalloped potatoes are creamy, cheesy, and full of flavor. Adjust the seasonings and cheese to suit your taste preferences.

Baked Potato Skins with Cheese and Bacon

Ingredients:

- 4 large russet potatoes
- 2 tablespoons olive oil
- Salt and pepper, to taste
- 1 cup shredded cheddar cheese
- 8 slices of cooked bacon, crumbled
- Sour cream, for serving
- Chopped green onions or chives, for garnish (optional)

Instructions:

Preheat the Oven:
- Preheat your oven to 400°F (200°C).

Bake the Potatoes:
- Wash and scrub the potatoes thoroughly. Pierce each potato several times with a fork. Rub them with olive oil, salt, and pepper.
- Place the potatoes directly on the oven rack and bake for about 45-60 minutes or until the potatoes are fork-tender.
- Remove the potatoes from the oven and let them cool slightly.

Prepare the Potato Skins:
- Cut the baked potatoes in half lengthwise. Scoop out the flesh, leaving about 1/4 inch of potato on the skin.
- Reserve the scooped-out potato for another use (e.g., mashed potatoes).

Brush with Olive Oil:
- Brush the inside and outside of each potato skin with olive oil. This helps make them crispy.

Bake Again:
- Place the potato skins on a baking sheet, skin side down. Bake in the preheated oven for about 10 minutes or until they start to crisp.

Add Cheese and Bacon:
- Remove the potato skins from the oven. Fill each skin with shredded cheddar cheese and crumbled bacon.

Bake Until Cheese Melts:
- Return the filled potato skins to the oven and bake for an additional 5-7 minutes or until the cheese is melted and bubbly.

Serve:

- Remove from the oven and let them cool slightly. Serve the baked potato skins with sour cream on the side.

Garnish and Enjoy:
- Garnish with chopped green onions or chives if desired. Serve these cheesy and bacon-filled delights as a crowd-pleasing appetizer.

These baked potato skins are a delightful combination of crispy, cheesy, and savory flavors. They're perfect for game nights, parties, or as an indulgent snack.

Hasselback Potatoes

Ingredients:

- 4 large russet potatoes
- 4 tablespoons unsalted butter, melted
- 2 tablespoons olive oil
- 2-3 cloves garlic, minced
- Salt and pepper, to taste
- Fresh herbs (rosemary or thyme), chopped (optional)
- Grated Parmesan cheese (optional)

Instructions:

Preheat the Oven:
- Preheat your oven to 425°F (220°C).

Prepare the Potatoes:
- Wash and scrub the potatoes thoroughly. Pat them dry with a paper towel.

Make Hasselback Cuts:
- Place a potato on a cutting board, flat side down. Starting from one end, make thin slices across the potato, making sure not to cut all the way through. Leave about 1/8 inch at the bottom, so the slices stay connected.

Garlic Butter Mixture:
- In a bowl, mix melted butter, olive oil, minced garlic, and salt. Optionally, add chopped fresh herbs like rosemary or thyme for added flavor.

Coat the Potatoes:
- Place the hasselback potatoes on a baking sheet. Brush the garlic butter mixture generously over each potato, making sure to get the mixture between the slices.

Bake:
- Bake in the preheated oven for about 45-55 minutes or until the potatoes are crispy on the outside and tender on the inside. Baste the potatoes with the butter mixture halfway through the baking time.

Optional Cheese Topping:
- If desired, sprinkle grated Parmesan cheese over the potatoes during the last 10-15 minutes of baking. This adds a delicious cheesy crust.

Serve:

- Once the potatoes are golden brown and crispy, remove them from the oven. Serve immediately.

Garnish and Enjoy:
- Garnish with additional herbs if desired. The hasselback potatoes are ready to be served as a visually appealing and flavorful side dish.

These hasselback potatoes are a perfect combination of crispy edges and a creamy interior. They make an elegant side dish for special occasions or a unique twist on the classic baked potato.

Potato Gnocchi with Sage Butter

Ingredients:

For the Potato Gnocchi:

- 2 large russet potatoes, baked or boiled until tender
- 1 egg, beaten
- 1 cup all-purpose flour, plus extra for dusting
- Salt, to taste

For the Sage Butter Sauce:

- 1/2 cup unsalted butter
- Fresh sage leaves
- Salt and pepper, to taste
- Grated Parmesan cheese, for serving (optional)

Instructions:

1. Prepare the Potato Gnocchi:

a. Once the potatoes are cooked and still warm, peel and mash them until smooth. Let them cool slightly.

b. Add the beaten egg and a pinch of salt to the mashed potatoes. Gradually incorporate the flour, mixing until a soft dough forms.

c. On a floured surface, divide the dough into manageable portions. Roll each portion into a long, thin rope, about 1/2 inch in diameter.

d. Cut the ropes into small pieces to form the gnocchi. You can use a fork to create ridges on each piece.

e. Place the gnocchi on a floured tray to prevent sticking.

2. Cook the Potato Gnocchi:

a. Bring a large pot of salted water to a boil.

b. Drop the gnocchi into the boiling water. They are cooked when they float to the surface, which usually takes 2-3 minutes.

c. Using a slotted spoon, transfer the cooked gnocchi to a plate.

3. Make Sage Butter Sauce:

a. In a large skillet, melt the butter over medium heat.

b. Add fresh sage leaves to the melted butter. Allow them to sizzle for about 1-2 minutes until fragrant and the butter starts to brown slightly.

c. Season the sage butter with salt and pepper to taste.

4. Combine and Serve:

a. Add the cooked gnocchi to the sage butter sauce. Toss gently to coat the gnocchi evenly.

b. Serve the Potato Gnocchi with Sage Butter immediately, optionally garnished with grated Parmesan cheese.

This dish is simple yet rich in flavor, with the nutty aroma of sage complementing the soft potato gnocchi. It makes for a delightful and comforting meal.

Loaded Potato Soup

Ingredients:

- 6 large russet potatoes, peeled and diced
- 6 slices bacon, cooked and crumbled
- 1 medium onion, finely chopped
- 3 cloves garlic, minced
- 4 cups chicken or vegetable broth
- 2 cups milk (whole milk or a combination of milk and cream)
- 1 cup shredded cheddar cheese
- 1/2 cup sour cream
- 1/4 cup all-purpose flour
- 2 tablespoons unsalted butter
- Salt and pepper, to taste
- Green onions, chopped, for garnish
- Additional shredded cheddar, for topping (optional)

Instructions:

Cook Bacon:
- In a large pot, cook the bacon until crispy. Remove the bacon, crumble it, and set aside. Reserve some for garnish.

Saute Onions and Garlic:
- In the same pot, drain excess bacon grease, leaving about 1 tablespoon. Saute the chopped onion until softened. Add minced garlic and cook for an additional 1-2 minutes.

Make Roux:
- Add butter to the pot and let it melt. Stir in the flour to create a roux. Cook for 2-3 minutes until it's lightly golden.

Add Broth and Potatoes:
- Gradually whisk in the chicken or vegetable broth to avoid lumps. Add diced potatoes, bring the mixture to a simmer, and cook until the potatoes are fork-tender.

Blend Soup:
- Using an immersion blender, blend the soup partially to achieve a creamy consistency while leaving some potato chunks for texture. If you don't have an immersion blender, you can transfer a portion of the soup to a blender and then return it to the pot.

Add Milk and Cheese:
- Stir in the milk, shredded cheddar cheese, and sour cream. Heat the soup until the cheese is melted and the soup is heated through. Season with salt and pepper to taste.

Serve:
- Ladle the loaded potato soup into bowls. Top each serving with crumbled bacon, chopped green onions, and additional shredded cheddar cheese if desired.

Enjoy:
- Serve the Loaded Potato Soup hot, and enjoy this comforting and satisfying bowl of goodness.

This loaded potato soup is a delightful combination of creamy, cheesy, and savory flavors. It's sure to become a favorite for cozy evenings at home.

Potato Pancakes (Latkes)

Ingredients:

- 6 large russet potatoes, peeled and diced
- 6 slices bacon, cooked and crumbled
- 1 medium onion, finely chopped
- 3 cloves garlic, minced
- 4 cups chicken or vegetable broth
- 2 cups milk (whole milk or a combination of milk and cream)
- 1 cup shredded cheddar cheese
- 1/2 cup sour cream
- 1/4 cup all-purpose flour
- 2 tablespoons unsalted butter
- Salt and pepper, to taste
- Green onions, chopped, for garnish
- Additional shredded cheddar, for topping (optional)

Instructions:

Cook Bacon:
- In a large pot, cook the bacon until crispy. Remove the bacon, crumble it, and set aside. Reserve some for garnish.

Saute Onions and Garlic:
- In the same pot, drain excess bacon grease, leaving about 1 tablespoon. Saute the chopped onion until softened. Add minced garlic and cook for an additional 1-2 minutes.

Make Roux:
- Add butter to the pot and let it melt. Stir in the flour to create a roux. Cook for 2-3 minutes until it's lightly golden.

Add Broth and Potatoes:
- Gradually whisk in the chicken or vegetable broth to avoid lumps. Add diced potatoes, bring the mixture to a simmer, and cook until the potatoes are fork-tender.

Blend Soup:
- Using an immersion blender, blend the soup partially to achieve a creamy consistency while leaving some potato chunks for texture. If you don't

have an immersion blender, you can transfer a portion of the soup to a blender and then return it to the pot.

Add Milk and Cheese:
- Stir in the milk, shredded cheddar cheese, and sour cream. Heat the soup until the cheese is melted and the soup is heated through. Season with salt and pepper to taste.

Serve:
- Ladle the loaded potato soup into bowls. Top each serving with crumbled bacon, chopped green onions, and additional shredded cheddar cheese if desired.

Enjoy:
- Serve the Loaded Potato Soup hot, and enjoy this comforting and satisfying bowl of goodness.

This loaded potato soup is a delightful combination of creamy, cheesy, and savory flavors. It's sure to become a favorite for cozy evenings at home.

Potatoes Au Gratin

Ingredients:

- 4 large russet potatoes, peeled and thinly sliced
- 2 cups heavy cream
- 2 cloves garlic, minced
- 2 cups shredded Gruyere cheese (or a combination of Gruyere and Swiss)
- 1 cup shredded Parmesan cheese
- Salt and pepper, to taste
- 1/2 teaspoon nutmeg (optional)
- Butter for greasing the baking dish
- Chopped fresh parsley for garnish (optional)

Instructions:

Preheat the Oven:
- Preheat your oven to 375°F (190°C). Butter a baking dish.

Prepare the Potatoes:
- Peel the potatoes and thinly slice them, preferably using a mandoline for even thickness.

Make the Cream Mixture:
- In a saucepan, heat the heavy cream and minced garlic over medium heat until it just begins to simmer. Remove from heat.

Layer Potatoes and Cheese:
- Arrange a layer of sliced potatoes in the buttered baking dish. Sprinkle with salt, pepper, and a bit of nutmeg if using. Add a layer of Gruyere and Parmesan cheese. Repeat the process, creating several layers.

Pour Cream Mixture:
- Pour the warm cream mixture over the layered potatoes and cheese. Press down gently to ensure the cream is distributed evenly.

Bake:
- Cover the baking dish with foil and bake in the preheated oven for about 45 minutes. Uncover and bake for an additional 20-30 minutes or until the top is golden brown, and the potatoes are tender.

Rest Before Serving:
- Allow the Potatoes Au Gratin to rest for 10-15 minutes before serving. This helps the dish set.

Garnish and Serve:
- Garnish with chopped fresh parsley if desired. Serve the Potatoes Au Gratin as a delectable side dish.

This dish is a perfect accompaniment to holiday meals or special occasions, providing a rich and satisfying combination of creamy potatoes and melted cheese.

Cheesy Twice-Baked Potatoes

Ingredients:

- 4 large russet potatoes
- 1/2 cup sour cream
- 1/4 cup unsalted butter, softened
- 1/2 cup milk
- 1 cup shredded cheddar cheese
- 1/2 cup chopped green onions
- Salt and pepper, to taste
- 1/2 cup grated Parmesan cheese
- Additional shredded cheddar and chopped green onions for topping (optional)

Instructions:

Preheat the Oven:
- Preheat your oven to 400°F (200°C).

Bake the Potatoes:
- Wash the potatoes and pierce them with a fork. Bake in the preheated oven for about 1 hour or until they are tender.

Prepare the Potatoes:
- Allow the baked potatoes to cool slightly. Cut each potato in half lengthwise.

Scoop and Mash:
- Scoop out the insides of the potatoes, leaving a thin layer attached to the skin. Place the potato flesh in a mixing bowl.
- Mash the potato flesh with a fork or potato masher.

Add Ingredients:
- To the mashed potatoes, add sour cream, softened butter, milk, shredded cheddar cheese, chopped green onions, salt, and pepper. Mix until well combined.

Refill the Potato Skins:
- Spoon the mashed potato mixture back into the potato skins.

Top with Cheese:
- Sprinkle grated Parmesan cheese over the top of each filled potato.

Bake Again:
- Place the filled potato halves on a baking sheet. Bake in the oven for an additional 15-20 minutes or until the tops are golden brown.

Optional Toppings:

- If desired, sprinkle additional shredded cheddar cheese and chopped green onions on top during the last 5 minutes of baking.

Serve:
- Remove from the oven and let the Cheesy Twice-Baked Potatoes cool for a few minutes before serving.

Enjoy:
- Serve these delicious and cheesy twice-baked potatoes as a delightful side dish.

These Cheesy Twice-Baked Potatoes are creamy, flavorful, and make for a fantastic accompaniment to a variety of main dishes. They're sure to be a hit at any meal!

International Flavors:

Spanish Patatas Bravas

Ingredients:

For the Potatoes:

- 4 large russet potatoes, peeled and cut into 1-inch cubes
- Olive oil for frying
- Salt, to taste

For the Bravas Sauce:

- 1 can (14 ounces) crushed tomatoes
- 2 cloves garlic, minced
- 1 teaspoon smoked paprika
- 1/2 teaspoon cayenne pepper (adjust to taste for spiciness)
- 1 teaspoon sugar
- Salt and black pepper, to taste
- 2 tablespoons olive oil

For the Garlic Aioli:

- 1/2 cup mayonnaise
- 2 cloves garlic, minced
- 1 tablespoon lemon juice
- Salt and pepper, to taste

For Garnish:

- Chopped fresh parsley

Instructions:

1. Prepare the Potatoes:

a. Heat olive oil in a large skillet or deep fryer to 350°F (175°C).

b. Fry the potato cubes in batches until golden brown and crispy. Remove with a slotted spoon and place them on a paper towel-lined plate. Season with salt.

2. Make the Bravas Sauce:

a. In a saucepan, heat olive oil over medium heat. Add minced garlic and cook for 1-2 minutes until fragrant.

b. Add crushed tomatoes, smoked paprika, cayenne pepper, sugar, salt, and black pepper. Simmer for 15-20 minutes, stirring occasionally, until the sauce thickens. Adjust seasoning to taste.

3. Prepare Garlic Aioli:

a. In a small bowl, mix together mayonnaise, minced garlic, lemon juice, salt, and pepper. Adjust the seasoning according to your taste.

4. Assemble and Serve:

a. Arrange the crispy potatoes on a serving platter.

b. Drizzle the bravas sauce over the potatoes.

c. Spoon dollops of garlic aioli on top.

d. Garnish with chopped fresh parsley.

5. Enjoy:

Serve Spanish Patatas Bravas immediately as a delicious and flavorful tapas dish.

These Patatas Bravas are known for their crispy exterior, soft interior, and the combination of the spicy bravas sauce with the creamy garlic aioli. They make for a fantastic appetizer or side dish.

Indian Aloo Gobi (Potato and Cauliflower)

Ingredients:

- 2 cups cauliflower florets
- 2 medium-sized potatoes, peeled and diced
- 1 large onion, finely chopped
- 2 tomatoes, finely chopped
- 1/2 cup frozen peas (optional)
- 2-3 tablespoons oil or ghee
- 1 teaspoon cumin seeds
- 1 teaspoon mustard seeds
- 1/2 teaspoon turmeric powder
- 1 teaspoon red chili powder (adjust to taste)
- 1 teaspoon ground coriander
- 1 teaspoon ground cumin
- 1 teaspoon garam masala
- Salt, to taste
- Fresh coriander leaves, chopped, for garnish

Instructions:

Prepare Vegetables:
- Wash and cut the cauliflower into small florets. Peel and dice the potatoes into small cubes. Rinse them thoroughly.

Heat Oil:
- In a large pan or kadai, heat oil or ghee over medium heat.

Tempering:
- Add cumin seeds and mustard seeds. Allow them to splutter.

Add Onions:
- Add finely chopped onions and sauté until they become translucent.

Spices:
- Stir in turmeric powder, red chili powder, ground coriander, ground cumin, and salt. Mix well to coat the onions in the spices.

Add Tomatoes:
- Add the chopped tomatoes and cook until they become soft and the oil begins to separate.

Add Potatoes and Cauliflower:
- Add the diced potatoes and cauliflower florets to the pan. Mix them well with the spice and tomato mixture.

Cover and Cook:
- Cover the pan with a lid and let the vegetables cook on low to medium heat. Stir occasionally to ensure even cooking.

Check Doneness:
- Once the potatoes and cauliflower are almost cooked, add frozen peas if using. Continue cooking until all the vegetables are tender but not mushy.

Garam Masala:
- Sprinkle garam masala over the cooked vegetables and give it a final mix.

Garnish and Serve:
- Garnish with chopped fresh coriander leaves.

Serve:
- Aloo Gobi is ready to be served. Enjoy it with naan, roti, or rice.

This Aloo Gobi recipe is a delightful combination of spices and textures, making it a popular and comforting dish in Indian cuisine.

Irish Colcannon

Ingredients:

- 4 large russet potatoes, peeled and cut into chunks
- 1/2 cup unsalted butter
- 1 cup chopped kale or cabbage
- 1 cup green onions, finely chopped (or use leeks for a milder flavor)
- 1 cup milk
- Salt and pepper, to taste
- Fresh parsley, chopped, for garnish (optional)

Instructions:

Boil Potatoes:
- Place the peeled and cut potatoes in a large pot of salted water. Bring to a boil and simmer until the potatoes are fork-tender.

Prepare Kale or Cabbage:
- While the potatoes are boiling, cook the chopped kale or cabbage in a separate pot of boiling water for about 5 minutes or until tender. Drain and set aside.

Make Mashed Potatoes:
- Drain the boiled potatoes and mash them with a potato masher or fork. Add half of the butter and milk gradually while mashing to achieve a creamy consistency.

Add Greens:
- Stir in the cooked kale or cabbage and chopped green onions or leeks into the mashed potatoes. Mix well.

Season:
- Season the colcannon with salt and pepper to taste. Adjust the butter and milk quantities to achieve your desired consistency.

Serve:
- Transfer the colcannon to a serving dish. Make a well in the center and add the remaining butter.

Garnish and Enjoy:
- Garnish with fresh chopped parsley if desired. Serve the Irish Colcannon hot as a side dish, traditionally enjoyed with a knob of butter melting in the center.

Irish Colcannon is a hearty and flavorful dish that combines the creaminess of mashed potatoes with the earthy taste of kale or cabbage. It's often served as a side dish during holidays like St. Patrick's Day or with a variety of main courses.

Greek Lemon Potatoes

Ingredients:

- 4 large potatoes, peeled and cut into wedges or chunks
- 1/3 cup olive oil
- 1/3 cup fresh lemon juice (about 2-3 lemons)
- 3 cloves garlic, minced
- 1 teaspoon dried oregano
- 1 teaspoon dried thyme
- Salt and pepper, to taste
- 1 cup chicken or vegetable broth
- Fresh parsley, chopped, for garnish (optional)

Instructions:

Preheat the Oven:
- Preheat your oven to 400°F (200°C).

Prepare Potatoes:
- Peel the potatoes and cut them into wedges or chunks, depending on your preference.

Make Marinade:
- In a bowl, whisk together olive oil, lemon juice, minced garlic, dried oregano, dried thyme, salt, and pepper.

Coat Potatoes:
- Place the potato wedges in a large baking dish. Pour the marinade over the potatoes and toss to coat them evenly.

Add Broth:
- Pour the chicken or vegetable broth into the baking dish. This helps keep the potatoes moist while baking.

Bake:
- Bake in the preheated oven for about 45-55 minutes or until the potatoes are golden brown and tender. Stir the potatoes halfway through the baking time to ensure even cooking.

Garnish and Serve:
- Once the potatoes are done, remove them from the oven. Garnish with fresh chopped parsley if desired.

Enjoy:

- Serve the Greek Lemon Potatoes as a delicious side dish alongside your favorite Greek-inspired main course or any protein of your choice.

These Greek Lemon Potatoes are bursting with citrusy and herby flavors, making them a perfect accompaniment to a variety of meals. They're a delightful addition to your repertoire of side dishes.

Japanese Sweet Potato Tempura

Ingredients:

For Sweet Potato Tempura:

- 2 medium-sized Japanese sweet potatoes
- 1 cup all-purpose flour
- 1 cup ice-cold water
- 1 egg yolk
- Ice cubes (for chilling the batter)
- Vegetable oil (for deep frying)

For Dipping Sauce:

- 1/4 cup soy sauce
- 1 tablespoon mirin (sweet rice wine)
- 1 teaspoon sugar
- 1/4 cup water
- Grated daikon radish for garnish (optional)

Instructions:

1. Prepare Sweet Potatoes:

a. Peel the sweet potatoes and cut them into thin slices, about 1/8 to 1/4 inch thick.

2. Make Tempura Batter:

a. In a mixing bowl, combine the all-purpose flour, ice-cold water, and egg yolk. Mix until just combined. It's okay if the batter is a bit lumpy.

b. Place a handful of ice cubes in the batter to keep it cold. Stir briefly to maintain the chill.

3. Heat Oil:

a. Heat vegetable oil in a deep fryer or a heavy-bottomed pot to 340-350°F (170-180°C).

4. Coat Sweet Potatoes:

a. Dip each sweet potato slice into the tempura batter, ensuring it is well-coated.

5. Fry Tempura:

a. Carefully place the coated sweet potato slices into the hot oil. Fry until they are golden brown and crispy, turning them once to ensure even cooking. This usually takes about 3-4 minutes.

b. Use a slotted spoon to remove the sweet potato tempura from the oil and place them on a paper towel to absorb excess oil.

6. Make Dipping Sauce:

a. In a small saucepan, combine soy sauce, mirin, sugar, and water. Heat over low heat until the sugar dissolves. Let it cool.

7. Serve:

a. Serve the sweet potato tempura hot with the dipping sauce on the side. Optionally, garnish with grated daikon radish.

8. Enjoy:

a. Enjoy the Japanese Sweet Potato Tempura as a delicious appetizer or snack.

These tempura-coated sweet potatoes are not only crispy and flavorful but also showcase the unique sweetness of Japanese sweet potatoes. The dipping sauce adds a savory touch to complete the experience.

French Gratin Dauphinois

Ingredients:

- 2 pounds (about 1 kg) potatoes, peeled and thinly sliced (use waxy potatoes like Yukon Gold or russet)

- 2 cups heavy cream
- 2 cloves garlic, minced
- 1 bay leaf
- 1/2 teaspoon nutmeg, freshly grated
- Salt and pepper, to taste
- 1 cup Gruyère or Emmental cheese, grated (optional, for topping)
- Butter for greasing the baking dish

Instructions:

Preheat the Oven:
- Preheat your oven to 375°F (190°C).

Prepare Potatoes:
- Peel and thinly slice the potatoes. You can use a mandoline for even slices.

Make Cream Mixture:
- In a saucepan, combine the heavy cream, minced garlic, bay leaf, nutmeg, salt, and pepper. Heat over medium heat until it's just about to simmer. Remove from heat and let it steep for 10-15 minutes to infuse the flavors.

Butter the Baking Dish:
- Grease a baking dish with butter. This will prevent the potatoes from sticking.

Layer Potatoes:
- Arrange a layer of sliced potatoes in the baking dish. Pour a portion of the cream mixture over the potatoes. Repeat until all potatoes and cream are used, finishing with a layer of cream on top.

Bake:
- Bake in the preheated oven for about 45-60 minutes or until the potatoes are golden brown, and a knife easily pierces through the layers. If you're using cheese, sprinkle it over the top during the last 15-20 minutes of baking.

Rest Before Serving:
- Allow the Gratin Dauphinois to rest for about 10 minutes before serving. This helps the dish set.

Serve:
- Scoop portions onto plates and serve the Gratin Dauphinois hot.

Enjoy:

- Enjoy this French classic as a delicious side dish, especially perfect for special occasions.

Gratin Dauphinois is known for its creamy texture and rich flavor. The combination of garlic, nutmeg, and cream makes it a delightful accompaniment to a variety of main dishes.

German Potato Salad

Ingredients:

- 2 pounds (about 1 kg) Yukon Gold or red potatoes, peeled and thinly sliced
- 6 slices bacon, chopped
- 1 large onion, finely chopped
- 1/4 cup apple cider vinegar
- 1/4 cup chicken or vegetable broth
- 2 tablespoons Dijon mustard
- 2 tablespoons granulated sugar
- Salt and pepper, to taste
- Chopped fresh parsley, for garnish

Instructions:

Boil Potatoes:
- Place the sliced potatoes in a large pot, cover with cold water, and add a pinch of salt. Bring to a boil and simmer until the potatoes are just tender. Drain and set aside.

Cook Bacon and Onion:
- In a large skillet over medium heat, cook the chopped bacon until it becomes crispy. Remove some of the bacon bits for garnish if desired. Add the finely chopped onion to the skillet and cook until it becomes translucent.

Make Vinaigrette:
- In a small bowl, whisk together apple cider vinegar, chicken or vegetable broth, Dijon mustard, sugar, salt, and pepper.

Combine Ingredients:
- Add the boiled and drained potatoes to the skillet with bacon and onions. Pour the vinaigrette over the potatoes and gently toss to coat evenly.

Warm Salad:
- Warm the potato salad on low heat, stirring gently, for a few minutes until the flavors meld and the salad is heated through.

Garnish and Serve:
- Garnish the German Potato Salad with chopped fresh parsley and reserved bacon bits. Adjust salt and pepper to taste.

Enjoy:
- Serve the warm German Potato Salad as a side dish with your favorite main course.

This German Potato Salad is characterized by its tangy and savory dressing, making it a flavorful and comforting addition to your meal. It's often served at gatherings, picnics, or alongside grilled meats.

Swedish Hasselback Sweet Potatoes

Ingredients:

- 4 medium-sized sweet potatoes
- 3 tablespoons olive oil or melted butter
- Salt and pepper, to taste
- 2 tablespoons breadcrumbs (optional, for added crispiness)
- Fresh herbs (such as rosemary or thyme), chopped, for garnish
- Grated Parmesan cheese (optional, for topping)

Instructions:

Preheat the Oven:
- Preheat your oven to 400°F (200°C).

Prepare Sweet Potatoes:
- Wash and scrub the sweet potatoes. Pat them dry with a paper towel.

Make Hasselback Cuts:
- Place a sweet potato on a cutting board. Slice thin, even cuts into the sweet potato, making sure not to cut all the way through. You can achieve this by placing the potato between two chopsticks or wooden spoons to act as a guide for your knife.

Brush with Olive Oil:
- Place the sliced sweet potatoes on a baking sheet. Brush each sweet potato with olive oil or melted butter, ensuring that the oil or butter gets between the slices.

Season:
- Sprinkle salt and pepper over the sweet potatoes. If you desire additional crispiness, sprinkle breadcrumbs between the slices.

Bake:
- Bake in the preheated oven for about 40-50 minutes or until the sweet potatoes are tender and the edges are crispy. You can baste the sweet potatoes with more oil or butter halfway through baking.

Optional Cheese Topping:
- If desired, sprinkle grated Parmesan cheese over the sweet potatoes during the last 10-15 minutes of baking. This adds a delicious cheesy crust.

Garnish and Serve:
- Remove the Swedish Hasselback Sweet Potatoes from the oven. Garnish with fresh chopped herbs, and serve them hot.

Enjoy:

- Enjoy these Hasselback Sweet Potatoes as a flavorful and visually stunning side dish.

These Hasselback Sweet Potatoes are not only a treat for the taste buds but also make an elegant presentation. They are perfect for holidays, family dinners, or any time you want to impress with a simple yet sophisticated dish.

Mexican Papas con Chorizo

Ingredients:

- 4 medium-sized potatoes, peeled and diced
- 1 pound (about 450g) fresh chorizo sausage, casings removed
- 1 onion, finely chopped
- 2 cloves garlic, minced
- 1 can (14 ounces) diced tomatoes, drained
- 1 jalapeño pepper, finely chopped (optional, for added heat)
- 1 teaspoon ground cumin
- Salt and pepper, to taste
- Fresh cilantro, chopped, for garnish
- Lime wedges, for serving
- Corn or flour tortillas, for serving

Instructions:

Cook Potatoes:
- Place the diced potatoes in a pot of salted water. Bring to a boil and simmer until the potatoes are just tender. Drain and set aside.

Cook Chorizo:
- In a large skillet, cook the chorizo over medium heat, breaking it up with a spoon as it cooks. Cook until the chorizo is browned and cooked through.

Add Aromatics:
- Add finely chopped onion and minced garlic to the skillet. Sauté until the onion is translucent.

Add Potatoes:
- Add the drained diced potatoes to the skillet with the chorizo mixture. Stir to combine.

Season:
- Season the mixture with ground cumin, salt, and pepper. Add the diced tomatoes and chopped jalapeño if using. Stir well to incorporate the flavors.

Simmer:
- Allow the Papas con Chorizo to simmer for about 10-15 minutes, allowing the flavors to meld and the potatoes to absorb the delicious chorizo seasoning.

Garnish and Serve:
- Garnish with fresh chopped cilantro. Serve the Papas con Chorizo hot with lime wedges and warm tortillas.

Enjoy:
- Enjoy this Mexican comfort food with the vibrant flavors of chorizo and potatoes.

Papas con Chorizo can be enjoyed as a filling for tacos, burritos, or served with warm tortillas on the side. It's a versatile dish that is sure to satisfy your taste buds with its bold and spicy flavors.

Italian Potato Gnocchi in Tomato Sauce

Ingredients:

For Potato Gnocchi:

- 2 pounds (about 900g) russet potatoes, peeled and boiled until fork-tender
- 1 large egg, beaten
- 2 cups all-purpose flour, plus extra for dusting
- Salt, to taste

For Tomato Sauce:

- 2 tablespoons olive oil
- 1 onion, finely chopped
- 2 cloves garlic, minced
- 1 can (28 ounces) crushed tomatoes
- 1 teaspoon dried oregano
- 1 teaspoon dried basil
- Salt and pepper, to taste
- Fresh basil leaves, chopped, for garnish (optional)
- Grated Parmesan cheese, for serving

Instructions:

1. Make Potato Gnocchi:

a. Mash the boiled potatoes while they are still warm, or use a potato ricer for a smoother texture.

b. Allow the mashed potatoes to cool slightly. Add the beaten egg and a pinch of salt. Gradually incorporate the flour, mixing until a soft dough forms.

c. On a floured surface, divide the dough into manageable portions. Roll each portion into a long, thin rope, about 1/2 inch in diameter.

d. Cut the ropes into small pieces, forming the gnocchi. You can use a fork to create ridges on each piece.

e. Place the gnocchi on a floured tray to prevent sticking.

2. Cook Potato Gnocchi:

a. Bring a large pot of salted water to a boil.

b. Drop the gnocchi into the boiling water. They are cooked when they float to the surface, usually taking about 2-3 minutes.

c. Using a slotted spoon, transfer the cooked gnocchi to a plate.

3. Make Tomato Sauce:

a. In a saucepan, heat olive oil over medium heat. Add finely chopped onion and sauté until it becomes translucent.

b. Add minced garlic and sauté for an additional minute.

c. Pour in the crushed tomatoes and add dried oregano, dried basil, salt, and pepper. Simmer the sauce for about 15-20 minutes, stirring occasionally, until it thickens.

4. Combine and Serve:

a. Add the cooked potato gnocchi to the tomato sauce. Toss gently to coat the gnocchi evenly.

b. Serve the Italian Potato Gnocchi in Tomato Sauce hot, garnished with fresh chopped basil if desired, and grated Parmesan cheese.

This dish is a delightful combination of pillowy potato gnocchi and a rich tomato sauce. It's a classic Italian comfort food that you can enjoy as a main course or side dish.

Healthy Potato Options:

Baked Sweet Potato Fries

Ingredients:

- 2 large sweet potatoes, peeled and cut into thin matchsticks or wedges
- 2 tablespoons olive oil
- 1 teaspoon paprika
- 1/2 teaspoon garlic powder
- 1/2 teaspoon onion powder
- 1/2 teaspoon cumin
- 1/2 teaspoon chili powder (adjust to taste for spiciness)
- Salt and pepper, to taste
- Optional: 1 tablespoon cornstarch (for extra crispiness)

Instructions:

Preheat the Oven:
- Preheat your oven to 425°F (220°C).

Prepare Sweet Potatoes:
- Peel the sweet potatoes and cut them into thin matchsticks or wedges, depending on your preference.

Soak in Water (Optional):
- If you have time, soak the cut sweet potatoes in cold water for about 30 minutes. This can help remove excess starch and make the fries crispier. Pat them dry thoroughly before proceeding.

Seasoning:
- In a large bowl, toss the sweet potato sticks with olive oil, paprika, garlic powder, onion powder, cumin, chili powder, salt, and pepper. Optional: Sprinkle cornstarch over the sweet potatoes and toss to coat evenly for extra crispiness.

Spread on Baking Sheet:
- Arrange the seasoned sweet potato fries in a single layer on a baking sheet. Make sure they are not crowded to allow for even baking.

Bake:
- Bake in the preheated oven for 25-30 minutes, turning the fries halfway through, or until they are golden brown and crispy.

Serve:
- Remove from the oven and let them cool slightly. Serve the baked sweet potato fries hot.

Enjoy:

- Enjoy the baked sweet potato fries on their own or with your favorite dipping sauce.

These baked sweet potato fries are a healthier alternative to deep-fried options, and the combination of spices adds a delicious flavor. They make a fantastic side dish or a satisfying snack.

Roasted Garlic Rosemary Sweet Potatoes

Ingredients:

- 3 large sweet potatoes, peeled and cut into cubes or wedges
- 3 tablespoons olive oil
- 4 cloves garlic, minced
- 1 tablespoon fresh rosemary, finely chopped (or 1 teaspoon dried rosemary)
- Salt and pepper, to taste
- Optional: 1-2 tablespoons honey or maple syrup for a touch of sweetness

Instructions:

Preheat the Oven:
- Preheat your oven to 425°F (220°C).

Prepare Sweet Potatoes:
- Peel the sweet potatoes and cut them into cubes or wedges, depending on your preference.

Mix the Seasonings:
- In a large bowl, combine olive oil, minced garlic, chopped rosemary, salt, and pepper. If you prefer a touch of sweetness, you can add honey or maple syrup.

Coat Sweet Potatoes:
- Add the sweet potato cubes or wedges to the bowl with the seasonings. Toss well to coat the sweet potatoes evenly.

Spread on Baking Sheet:
- Spread the seasoned sweet potatoes in a single layer on a baking sheet. Make sure they are not overcrowded for even roasting.

Roast:
- Roast in the preheated oven for 25-30 minutes or until the sweet potatoes are tender and golden brown, turning them halfway through for even cooking.

Serve:
- Remove from the oven and transfer the roasted sweet potatoes to a serving dish.

Garnish and Enjoy:
- Garnish with additional fresh rosemary if desired. Serve the Roasted Garlic Rosemary Sweet Potatoes hot as a delicious side dish.

These roasted sweet potatoes are not only tasty but also fragrant with the combination of garlic and rosemary. They make a perfect accompaniment to a variety of main dishes and are great for holiday meals or everyday dinners.

Grilled Potato Skewers with Herbs

Ingredients:

- 2 pounds (about 900g) small potatoes (red or Yukon Gold), washed and halved
- 3 tablespoons olive oil
- 2 cloves garlic, minced
- 1 tablespoon fresh herbs (such as rosemary, thyme, or oregano), chopped
- Salt and pepper, to taste
- Wooden or metal skewers

Instructions:

Parboil Potatoes:
- Place the potato halves in a pot of salted boiling water and cook for about 5-7 minutes until they are just beginning to soften. You don't want them fully cooked at this stage.

Prepare Skewers:
- If using wooden skewers, soak them in water for about 30 minutes to prevent burning during grilling.

Marinate Potatoes:
- In a bowl, mix together olive oil, minced garlic, chopped herbs, salt, and pepper. Drain the partially cooked potatoes and toss them in the herb-infused oil mixture until they are well coated.

Skewer Potatoes:
- Thread the marinated potato halves onto the skewers, ensuring they are close together but not too tightly packed.

Preheat Grill:
- Preheat your grill to medium-high heat.

Grill:
- Place the skewers on the preheated grill. Grill for about 15-20 minutes, turning occasionally, until the potatoes are tender and have nice grill marks.

Serve:
- Remove the skewers from the grill and transfer them to a serving platter.

Garnish and Enjoy:
- Garnish with additional fresh herbs if desired. Serve the Grilled Potato Skewers hot as a tasty side dish.

These Grilled Potato Skewers with Herbs are not only delicious but also visually appealing. They are perfect for summer barbecues, picnics, or as a side dish for any grilled main course.

Spiralized Potato Noodles with Pesto

Ingredients:

For Potato Noodles:

- 4 medium-sized potatoes, washed and peeled
- 2 tablespoons olive oil
- Salt and pepper, to taste

For Pesto:

- 2 cups fresh basil leaves, packed
- 1/2 cup grated Parmesan cheese
- 1/3 cup pine nuts or walnuts
- 2 cloves garlic, peeled
- 1/2 cup extra-virgin olive oil
- Salt and pepper, to taste
- 1/2 cup grated Pecorino Romano cheese (optional, for extra flavor)

Instructions:

1. Make Pesto:

a. In a food processor, combine fresh basil, Parmesan cheese, pine nuts or walnuts, and garlic.

b. Pulse until the ingredients are finely chopped.

c. With the food processor running, slowly pour in the olive oil until the pesto reaches your desired consistency.

d. Season with salt and pepper to taste. If you like, you can add grated Pecorino Romano cheese for an extra layer of flavor.

2. Spiralize Potatoes:

a. Use a spiralizer to turn the peeled potatoes into long, spiralized noodles.

b. If you don't have a spiralizer, you can use a vegetable peeler to create ribbon-like strips.

3. Cook Potato Noodles:

a. Heat 2 tablespoons of olive oil in a large skillet over medium heat.

b. Add the spiralized potato noodles to the skillet. Season with salt and pepper.

c. Sauté the potato noodles for 5-7 minutes, or until they are cooked through and slightly crispy on the edges.

4. Combine Potato Noodles with Pesto:

a. Once the potato noodles are cooked, remove them from the heat.

b. Add a generous amount of pesto to the skillet with the potato noodles. Toss gently until the noodles are well coated with the pesto.

5. Serve:

a. Transfer the Spiralized Potato Noodles with Pesto to a serving dish.

b. Optionally, garnish with additional grated Parmesan cheese and fresh basil.

6. Enjoy:

a. Serve immediately and enjoy your delicious Spiralized Potato Noodles with Pesto.

This dish is not only visually appealing but also a tasty way to enjoy potatoes in a unique form. The vibrant green pesto adds a burst of flavor to the spiralized potato noodles.

Sweet Potato and Black Bean Stuffed Peppers

Ingredients:

- 4 large bell peppers, halved and seeds removed
- 1 cup quinoa, cooked according to package instructions

- 1 large sweet potato, peeled and diced
- 1 can (15 ounces) black beans, drained and rinsed
- 1 cup corn kernels (fresh or frozen)
- 1 cup diced tomatoes
- 1 cup shredded cheese (cheddar, Monterey Jack, or your choice)
- 2 cloves garlic, minced
- 1 teaspoon ground cumin
- 1 teaspoon chili powder
- Salt and pepper, to taste
- Olive oil, for drizzling
- Fresh cilantro, chopped, for garnish (optional)
- Lime wedges, for serving

Instructions:

Preheat the Oven:
- Preheat your oven to 375°F (190°C).

Prepare Bell Peppers:
- Cut the bell peppers in half lengthwise, and remove the seeds and membranes. Place the pepper halves in a baking dish.

Roast Sweet Potatoes:
- Toss the diced sweet potatoes with olive oil, salt, and pepper. Roast in the oven for about 20-25 minutes or until tender.

Prepare Filling:
- In a large bowl, combine the cooked quinoa, roasted sweet potatoes, black beans, corn, diced tomatoes, shredded cheese, minced garlic, ground cumin, chili powder, salt, and pepper. Mix well.

Stuff Peppers:
- Spoon the filling into each bell pepper half, pressing it down gently.

Bake:
- Cover the baking dish with aluminum foil and bake in the preheated oven for 25-30 minutes, or until the peppers are tender.

Broil (Optional):
- If you'd like to brown the tops, remove the foil and broil for an additional 3-5 minutes until the filling is golden.

Garnish and Serve:

- Remove from the oven and garnish with fresh cilantro if desired. Serve the Sweet Potato and Black Bean Stuffed Peppers with lime wedges on the side.

Enjoy:

- Enjoy these delicious stuffed peppers as a satisfying and wholesome meal.

These stuffed peppers are packed with a combination of sweet and savory flavors. They make a perfect vegetarian dish for a healthy and hearty dinner.

Crispy Oven-Baked Potato Wedges

Ingredients:

- 4 large russet potatoes, washed and scrubbed
- 2 tablespoons olive oil
- 1 teaspoon garlic powder
- 1 teaspoon onion powder
- 1 teaspoon paprika
- 1/2 teaspoon dried thyme
- Salt and pepper, to taste
- Optional: Parmesan cheese, grated, for garnish
- Fresh parsley, chopped, for garnish

Instructions:

Preheat the Oven:
- Preheat your oven to 425°F (220°C).

Prepare Potatoes:
- Scrub the potatoes thoroughly, leaving the skin on. Cut each potato into wedges.

Soak Potatoes (Optional):
- If you have time, soak the potato wedges in cold water for about 30 minutes. This helps remove excess starch and can contribute to crispier wedges. Pat them dry with a paper towel before proceeding.

Seasoning:
- In a large bowl, toss the potato wedges with olive oil, garlic powder, onion powder, paprika, dried thyme, salt, and pepper. Make sure the wedges are evenly coated.

Arrange on Baking Sheet:
- Place the seasoned potato wedges in a single layer on a baking sheet. Ensure they are not overcrowded to allow for even baking.

Bake:
- Bake in the preheated oven for 30-35 minutes, flipping the wedges halfway through, or until they are golden brown and crispy.

Optional Cheese Garnish:
- If you like, sprinkle grated Parmesan cheese over the wedges during the last 5 minutes of baking for a cheesy crust.

Garnish and Serve:
- Once baked, remove the potato wedges from the oven. Garnish with fresh chopped parsley.

Enjoy:

- Serve the crispy oven-baked potato wedges hot as a delightful side dish or snack.

These potato wedges are crispy on the outside and tender on the inside, making them a perfect accompaniment to burgers, sandwiches, or enjoyed on their own with your favorite dipping sauce.

Greek Yogurt Potato Salad

Ingredients:

- 2 pounds (about 900g) red or Yukon Gold potatoes, washed and diced
- 1/2 cup Greek yogurt
- 2 tablespoons mayonnaise
- 1 tablespoon Dijon mustard
- 2 tablespoons fresh dill, chopped
- 1/4 cup red onion, finely chopped
- 1/4 cup celery, finely chopped
- Salt and pepper, to taste
- Optional: Lemon zest for added freshness

Instructions:

Boil Potatoes:
- Place the diced potatoes in a pot of cold, salted water. Bring to a boil and simmer until the potatoes are fork-tender. Drain and let them cool to room temperature.

Prepare Dressing:
- In a bowl, mix together Greek yogurt, mayonnaise, Dijon mustard, chopped dill, red onion, and celery. If you like, add a bit of lemon zest for extra freshness.

Combine Potatoes and Dressing:
- Gently fold the cooled diced potatoes into the Greek yogurt dressing mixture until the potatoes are well-coated.

Season:
- Season the potato salad with salt and pepper to taste. Adjust the seasoning as needed.

Chill:
- Cover the bowl with plastic wrap and refrigerate for at least 1-2 hours to allow the flavors to meld and the potato salad to chill.

Serve:
- Before serving, give the potato salad a gentle toss. Garnish with additional dill if desired.

Enjoy:
- Serve the Greek Yogurt Potato Salad chilled as a refreshing and healthier side dish.

This Greek Yogurt Potato Salad is a great alternative to traditional mayonnaise-based potato salads. It's light, creamy, and filled with the fresh flavors of dill and Greek yogurt. Perfect for picnics, barbecues, or as a side dish for any occasion.

Sweet Potato and Quinoa Patties

Ingredients:

- 1 cup quinoa, cooked according to package instructions
- 2 medium-sized sweet potatoes, peeled and grated
- 1/2 cup breadcrumbs
- 1/4 cup finely chopped red onion
- 2 cloves garlic, minced
- 1 teaspoon ground cumin
- 1 teaspoon paprika
- Salt and pepper, to taste
- 2 tablespoons chopped fresh cilantro or parsley
- 2 tablespoons olive oil (for cooking)
- Optional toppings: Greek yogurt, avocado slices, or your favorite sauce

Instructions:

Prepare Quinoa:
- Cook quinoa according to package instructions. Once cooked, let it cool to room temperature.

Grate Sweet Potatoes:
- Peel and grate the sweet potatoes using a box grater or a food processor.

Combine Ingredients:
- In a large mixing bowl, combine the cooked quinoa, grated sweet potatoes, breadcrumbs, chopped red onion, minced garlic, ground cumin, paprika, salt, pepper, and chopped cilantro or parsley. Mix well to combine.

Form Patties:
- Take a portion of the mixture and shape it into a patty with your hands. Repeat until all the mixture is used.

Chill (Optional):
- For firmer patties, you can refrigerate them for about 30 minutes before cooking.

Cook Patties:
- Heat olive oil in a skillet over medium heat. Once the oil is hot, add the patties and cook for about 4-5 minutes on each side or until they are golden brown and cooked through.

Serve:
- Transfer the sweet potato and quinoa patties to a serving plate.

Top and Enjoy:
- Top the patties with your choice of toppings, such as Greek yogurt, avocado slices, or your favorite sauce.

Enjoy:

- Serve the Sweet Potato and Quinoa Patties as a delicious and wholesome vegetarian meal.

These patties are not only packed with flavor but also offer a good dose of fiber and nutrients. They make a great option for lunch, dinner, or even as a meatless burger alternative.

Spicy Roasted Potatoes

Ingredients:

- 2 pounds (about 900g) potatoes, washed and diced into bite-sized pieces
- 3 tablespoons olive oil
- 1 teaspoon paprika
- 1/2 teaspoon cayenne pepper (adjust to taste for spiciness)
- 1 teaspoon garlic powder
- 1 teaspoon onion powder
- 1 teaspoon dried thyme
- Salt and pepper, to taste
- Fresh parsley, chopped, for garnish (optional)

Instructions:

Preheat the Oven:
- Preheat your oven to 425°F (220°C).

Prepare Potatoes:
- Wash and dice the potatoes into bite-sized pieces. Leave the skin on for added texture.

Seasoning:
- In a large bowl, combine the diced potatoes with olive oil, paprika, cayenne pepper, garlic powder, onion powder, dried thyme, salt, and pepper. Toss until the potatoes are evenly coated with the spices.

Spread on Baking Sheet:
- Spread the seasoned potatoes in a single layer on a baking sheet. Ensure they are not overcrowded for even roasting.

Roast:
- Roast in the preheated oven for about 30-35 minutes, turning the potatoes halfway through, or until they are golden brown and crispy.

Garnish:
- Once roasted, remove the potatoes from the oven. Garnish with fresh chopped parsley if desired.

Serve:
- Serve the spicy roasted potatoes hot as a delicious and flavorful side dish.

These spicy roasted potatoes are perfect for adding a kick to your meal. They make a great side dish for a variety of main courses, or you can enjoy them on their own with your favorite dipping sauce. Adjust the level of spiciness to suit your taste preferences.

Vegan Loaded Sweet Potato

Ingredients:

- 4 medium-sized sweet potatoes
- 1 can (15 ounces) black beans, drained and rinsed
- 1 cup corn kernels (fresh, frozen, or canned)
- 1 avocado, sliced
- 1 cup cherry tomatoes, halved
- 1/4 cup red onion, finely chopped
- Fresh cilantro, chopped, for garnish
- Lime wedges, for serving

Optional Toppings:

- Vegan cheese (shredded)
- Vegan sour cream
- Salsa
- Jalapeño slices
- Hot sauce
- Green onions, chopped

Instructions:

Bake Sweet Potatoes:
- Preheat your oven to 400°F (200°C). Wash and scrub the sweet potatoes, then pierce them with a fork. Place them on a baking sheet and bake for about 45-60 minutes, or until they are tender and easily pierced with a fork.

Prepare Toppings:
- While the sweet potatoes are baking, prepare your toppings. Drain and rinse the black beans, slice the avocado, halve the cherry tomatoes, chop the red onion, and gather any additional toppings you'd like to include.

Assemble Loaded Sweet Potatoes:
- Once the sweet potatoes are done, let them cool slightly. Cut a slit in the top and fluff the insides with a fork. Be careful not to cut through the bottom.
- Fill each sweet potato with a portion of black beans, corn, avocado slices, cherry tomatoes, and red onion.

Add Optional Toppings:
- Sprinkle with vegan cheese if desired and place the loaded sweet potatoes back in the oven for a few minutes to melt the cheese.

Garnish and Serve:

- Remove from the oven and garnish with chopped cilantro. Serve the Vegan Loaded Sweet Potatoes with lime wedges on the side.

Optional: Additional Toppings:
- Add a dollop of vegan sour cream, salsa, jalapeño slices, hot sauce, or chopped green onions.

Enjoy:
- Serve the Vegan Loaded Sweet Potatoes immediately and enjoy this nutritious and flavorful meal.

This dish is versatile, and you can get creative with your toppings based on your preferences. It's a satisfying and wholesome option for a vegan meal.

Breakfast and Brunch:

Potato and Spinach Breakfast Casserole

Ingredients:

- 4 cups potatoes, peeled and diced
- 1 tablespoon olive oil
- 1 small onion, finely chopped
- 2 cloves garlic, minced
- 4 cups fresh spinach, chopped
- 8 large eggs
- 1 cup milk (dairy or non-dairy)
- 1 cup shredded cheese (cheddar, mozzarella, or your choice)
- Salt and pepper, to taste
- 1 teaspoon dried thyme or your favorite herbs
- Optional: Sliced cherry tomatoes for garnish
- Fresh parsley, chopped, for garnish

Instructions:

Preheat the Oven:
- Preheat your oven to 375°F (190°C).

Prepare Potatoes:
- Peel and dice the potatoes into small cubes. Place them in a pot of salted water and boil until they are just fork-tender. Drain and set aside.

Sauté Vegetables:
- In a large skillet, heat olive oil over medium heat. Add chopped onions and sauté until they become translucent. Add minced garlic and cook for an additional minute.
- Add chopped spinach to the skillet and cook until it wilts. Remove from heat.

Assemble Casserole:
- In a greased baking dish, spread the boiled potatoes evenly. Top with the sautéed spinach and onion mixture.

Whisk Eggs and Milk:
- In a bowl, whisk together eggs, milk, salt, pepper, and dried thyme.

Pour Egg Mixture:
- Pour the egg mixture over the potatoes and spinach in the baking dish. Ensure it's evenly distributed.

Add Cheese:
- Sprinkle shredded cheese over the top of the casserole.

Bake:
- Bake in the preheated oven for 30-35 minutes or until the eggs are set, and the top is golden brown.

Garnish and Serve:
- Remove from the oven and let it cool slightly. Garnish with sliced cherry tomatoes and chopped fresh parsley.

Slice and Enjoy:
- Slice the Potato and Spinach Breakfast Casserole into squares or wedges and serve warm.

This casserole is not only delicious but also versatile. You can customize it by adding other vegetables, herbs, or your favorite spices. It's a great dish to prepare ahead of time for a crowd or for easy breakfasts throughout the week.

Hash Browns with Bell Peppers and Onions

Ingredients:

- 4 cups frozen shredded hash browns, thawed
- 1 bell pepper, diced (any color)
- 1 onion, diced
- 2 tablespoons olive oil
- Salt and pepper, to taste
- Optional: 1/2 teaspoon garlic powder or paprika for added flavor
- Fresh parsley, chopped, for garnish

Instructions:

Thaw Hash Browns:
- If using frozen hash browns, make sure to thaw them according to the package instructions. You can also use fresh shredded potatoes.

Sauté Vegetables:
- In a large skillet, heat olive oil over medium heat. Add diced bell peppers and onions. Sauté until they are softened and slightly caramelized.

Add Hash Browns:
- Add the thawed hash browns to the skillet, spreading them out evenly. Press them down with a spatula to form an even layer.

Season:
- Sprinkle salt, pepper, and optional garlic powder or paprika over the hash browns.

Cook:
- Let the hash browns cook without stirring for a few minutes to develop a crispy bottom. Then, gently flip sections of the hash browns to crisp the other side.

Continue Cooking:
- Continue cooking and flipping the hash browns until they are golden brown and crispy on the edges.

Garnish:
- Garnish with chopped fresh parsley for added freshness.

Serve:
- Serve the Hash Browns with Bell Peppers and Onions hot as a delicious and satisfying breakfast or side dish.

Feel free to customize the recipe by adding your favorite herbs, spices, or even cheese. These hash browns pair well with eggs, breakfast meats, or can be enjoyed on their own.

Sweet Potato Hash with Poached Eggs

Ingredients:

- 2 medium-sized sweet potatoes, peeled and diced
- 1 bell pepper, diced (any color)
- 1 small onion, finely chopped
- 2 tablespoons olive oil
- 1 teaspoon smoked paprika
- 1 teaspoon cumin
- Salt and pepper, to taste
- 4 large eggs
- Fresh cilantro or parsley, chopped, for garnish (optional)
- Avocado slices, for serving (optional)
- Hot sauce, for serving (optional)

Instructions:

Prepare Sweet Potatoes:
- Peel and dice the sweet potatoes into small, evenly sized cubes.

Sauté Vegetables:
- In a large skillet, heat olive oil over medium heat. Add chopped onions and sauté until they become translucent. Add diced sweet potatoes and bell pepper.

Season:
- Sprinkle smoked paprika, cumin, salt, and pepper over the sweet potatoes and bell pepper. Stir to coat the vegetables evenly with the spices.

Cook:
- Cook the sweet potato mixture, stirring occasionally, until the sweet potatoes are tender and slightly crispy on the edges. This usually takes about 15-20 minutes.

Poach Eggs:
- While the sweet potatoes are cooking, poach the eggs. Bring a pot of water to a gentle simmer. Crack each egg into a small bowl and gently slide it into the simmering water. Poach for about 3-4 minutes for a runny yolk.

Assemble:

- Divide the sweet potato hash among plates. Top each serving with a poached egg.

Garnish:
- Garnish with chopped cilantro or parsley. Add avocado slices if desired.

Serve:
- Serve the Sweet Potato Hash with Poached Eggs immediately, with hot sauce on the side if you like an extra kick.

This dish is not only visually appealing but also packed with flavors and nutrients. It makes a satisfying and wholesome breakfast or brunch option.

Irish Boxty (Potato Pancakes)

Ingredients:

- 2 cups grated raw potatoes
- 1 cup mashed potatoes (leftover or freshly mashed)
- 1 cup all-purpose flour
- 1 cup buttermilk
- 1 egg
- 1 small onion, finely chopped (optional)
- Salt and pepper, to taste
- Butter or oil for frying

Instructions:

Grate Potatoes:
- Peel and grate the raw potatoes. Place the grated potatoes in a clean kitchen towel and squeeze out any excess moisture.

Mix Ingredients:
- In a large mixing bowl, combine the grated potatoes, mashed potatoes, flour, buttermilk, egg, and chopped onion (if using). Mix well until a batter is formed.

Season:
- Season the batter with salt and pepper to taste. The amount of salt can vary depending on personal preference.

Rest the Batter:
- Allow the batter to rest for about 15-20 minutes. This helps the flour absorb the liquid and results in a better texture.

Cooking:
- Heat a skillet or griddle over medium heat. Add a bit of butter or oil to coat the surface.
- Spoon portions of the batter onto the hot skillet to form pancakes. Use the back of the spoon to spread the batter into a round shape.
- Cook each side until golden brown, about 3-4 minutes per side.

Serve:
- Serve the Irish Boxty hot with your favorite toppings. Common toppings include sour cream, applesauce, or a sprinkle of salt.

Optional: Keep Warm in Oven:

- If making a large batch, you can keep the cooked boxty warm in a low-temperature oven while you finish the rest.

Enjoy:
- Enjoy these Irish Boxty as a side dish or a main course. They are particularly popular for breakfast or brunch.

Irish Boxty is a versatile dish, and you can adjust the thickness of the pancakes based on your preference. Some variations also include adding herbs or additional ingredients for extra flavor.

Breakfast Stuffed Potatoes

Ingredients:

- 4 large baking potatoes
- 6 eggs
- 1/4 cup milk
- 1 cup diced bell peppers (mixed colors)
- 1 cup diced onions
- 1 cup diced tomatoes
- 1 cup shredded cheese (cheddar, Monterey Jack, or your choice)
- Salt and pepper, to taste
- 2 tablespoons olive oil
- Fresh chives or parsley, chopped, for garnish

Instructions:

Bake Potatoes:
- Preheat your oven to 400°F (200°C). Wash and scrub the potatoes, then pierce them with a fork. Bake the potatoes directly on the oven rack for about 45-60 minutes, or until they are tender when pierced with a fork.

Prepare Filling:
- While the potatoes are baking, prepare the filling. In a skillet, heat olive oil over medium heat. Add diced onions and bell peppers. Sauté until they are softened.

Scramble Eggs:
- In a bowl, whisk together eggs and milk. Pour the egg mixture into the skillet with the sautéed vegetables. Cook, stirring gently, until the eggs are scrambled and cooked to your liking.

Add Tomatoes and Season:
- Add diced tomatoes to the scrambled eggs. Season the mixture with salt and pepper to taste. Cook for an additional 1-2 minutes until the tomatoes are heated through.

Cut and Scoop Potatoes:
- Once the baked potatoes are done, let them cool slightly. Cut a slit in the top of each potato and scoop out some of the flesh to make room for the filling.

Fill Potatoes:

- Spoon the scrambled egg and vegetable mixture into each baked potato, filling them generously.

Top with Cheese:
- Sprinkle shredded cheese on top of each stuffed potato.

Broil (Optional):
- If you'd like to melt and brown the cheese, place the stuffed potatoes under the broiler for a couple of minutes until the cheese is bubbly and golden.

Garnish:
- Garnish the Breakfast Stuffed Potatoes with chopped fresh chives or parsley.

Serve:
- Serve the stuffed potatoes hot and enjoy a delicious breakfast!

These stuffed potatoes are customizable, so feel free to add other ingredients like cooked bacon, sausage, or your favorite herbs for extra flavor.

Cheesy Potato and Bacon Breakfast Burritos

Ingredients:

- 4 large flour tortillas
- 3 cups frozen shredded hash browns, cooked according to package instructions
- 8 slices bacon, cooked and crumbled
- 6 large eggs, scrambled
- 1 cup shredded cheddar cheese
- Salt and pepper, to taste
- 1/2 cup salsa (optional, for serving)
- Fresh cilantro, chopped, for garnish (optional)
- Sour cream or hot sauce (optional, for serving)

Instructions:

Cook Hash Browns:
- Cook the frozen shredded hash browns according to the package instructions until they are crispy and golden brown.

Cook Bacon:
- Cook the bacon until crispy. Once cooked, crumble or chop it into small pieces.

Scramble Eggs:
- In a bowl, whisk the eggs and season with salt and pepper. Scramble the eggs in a skillet over medium heat until they are just set.

Assemble Burritos:
- Warm the flour tortillas in a dry skillet or microwave for a few seconds to make them pliable.
- In the center of each tortilla, layer the cooked hash browns, scrambled eggs, crumbled bacon, and shredded cheddar cheese.

Fold and Roll:
- Fold the sides of the tortilla in towards the center, then roll from the bottom to create a burrito.

Serve:
- Place the burritos seam-side down on a serving plate. If you like, you can heat them in the skillet for a minute on each side to melt the cheese and crisp up the tortilla.

Garnish and Sauce:

- Garnish with fresh cilantro if desired. Serve with salsa, sour cream, or hot sauce on the side.

Enjoy:
- Enjoy the Cheesy Potato and Bacon Breakfast Burritos immediately while warm.

Feel free to customize these burritos with additional ingredients such as sautéed vegetables, avocado slices, or your favorite breakfast toppings. They make a convenient and tasty breakfast option for busy mornings.

Spanish Potato Omelette (Tortilla Española)

Ingredients:

- 4 large potatoes, peeled and thinly sliced
- 1 large onion, thinly sliced
- 6 large eggs
- Salt and pepper, to taste
- Olive oil for frying

Instructions:

Prepare Potatoes and Onions:
- Peel and thinly slice the potatoes and onions. The slices should be uniform for even cooking.

Fry Potatoes and Onions:
- In a large skillet, heat a generous amount of olive oil over medium heat. Add the sliced potatoes and onions. Cook them slowly, turning occasionally, until the potatoes are tender but not browned. This process is known as "confit" and can take about 15-20 minutes.

Drain Excess Oil:
- Once the potatoes and onions are cooked, remove them from the skillet, allowing excess oil to drain. You can place them in a colander or on paper towels.

Whisk Eggs:
- In a large bowl, whisk the eggs and season with salt and pepper.

Combine Eggs with Potatoes and Onions:
- Gently fold the cooked potatoes and onions into the whisked eggs, ensuring they are well coated.

Cook the Omelette:
- In the same skillet, add a bit more olive oil if needed. Pour the egg, potato, and onion mixture back into the skillet. Cook over medium-low heat, allowing the edges to set.
- Once the edges are set but the center is still slightly runny, place a flat plate over the skillet. Invert the omelette onto the plate.

Flip and Cook the Other Side:
- Slide the partially cooked side back into the skillet, allowing the other side to cook. You can use a spatula to help shape the edges.

Finish Cooking:

- Cook until the omelette is fully set and has a golden-brown color on both sides. The center should remain moist.

Serve:
- Slide the finished Tortilla Española onto a serving plate. Allow it to cool for a few minutes before slicing into wedges.

Enjoy:
- Serve the Spanish Potato Omelette warm or at room temperature. It's a classic tapas dish and can be enjoyed on its own or with a side of crusty bread.

Tortilla Española is a versatile dish, and variations may include ingredients like bell peppers or chorizo. This recipe provides the basic technique for the classic version.

Loaded Sweet Potato Breakfast Bowl

Ingredients:

- 2 medium-sized sweet potatoes
- 1 tablespoon olive oil
- Salt and pepper, to taste
- 2 cups baby spinach or kale, chopped
- 4 eggs
- 1 avocado, sliced
- 1/4 cup feta cheese, crumbled (optional)
- 1/4 cup cherry tomatoes, halved
- Hot sauce or salsa, for drizzling (optional)
- Fresh cilantro or parsley, chopped, for garnish

Instructions:

Preheat the Oven:
- Preheat your oven to 400°F (200°C).

Prepare Sweet Potatoes:
- Wash and scrub the sweet potatoes. Cut them into cubes, toss with olive oil, salt, and pepper. Spread them on a baking sheet in a single layer.

Roast Sweet Potatoes:
- Roast the sweet potatoes in the preheated oven for about 20-25 minutes or until they are tender and lightly browned, tossing halfway through.

Sauté Greens:
- While the sweet potatoes are roasting, sauté chopped baby spinach or kale in a pan with a bit of olive oil until wilted. Season with salt and pepper.

Cook Eggs:
- In the same pan, cook four eggs to your liking (scrambled, fried, or poached).

Assemble the Bowl:
- Divide the roasted sweet potatoes among serving bowls. Top with sautéed greens, cooked eggs, avocado slices, crumbled feta (if using), and cherry tomatoes.

Drizzle and Garnish:
- Drizzle hot sauce or salsa over the bowl if you like a bit of heat. Garnish with chopped fresh cilantro or parsley.

Enjoy:
- Serve the Loaded Sweet Potato Breakfast Bowl immediately and enjoy a nutritious and delicious breakfast.

Feel free to customize the bowl with additional toppings like black beans, sliced radishes, or a dollop of Greek yogurt. This breakfast bowl is a great way to incorporate a variety of flavors and textures into your morning meal.

Southwest Potato and Egg Skillet

Ingredients:

- 2 large potatoes, diced
- 1 tablespoon olive oil
- 1 small onion, diced
- 1 bell pepper (any color), diced
- 1 jalapeño, seeded and finely chopped (optional, for heat)
- 2 cloves garlic, minced
- 1 teaspoon ground cumin
- 1 teaspoon chili powder
- Salt and pepper, to taste
- 4 large eggs
- 1 cup black beans, cooked and drained
- 1 cup cherry tomatoes, halved
- 1/2 cup shredded cheddar cheese
- Fresh cilantro, chopped, for garnish
- Avocado slices, for serving (optional)
- Lime wedges, for serving

Instructions:

Cook Potatoes:
- In a large skillet, heat olive oil over medium heat. Add diced potatoes and cook until they are golden brown and cooked through. This may take about 10-15 minutes.

Add Vegetables:
- Add diced onion, bell pepper, jalapeño (if using), and minced garlic to the skillet. Sauté until the vegetables are softened.

Season:
- Sprinkle ground cumin, chili powder, salt, and pepper over the potato and vegetable mixture. Stir to coat evenly.

Create Wells for Eggs:
- Using a spatula, make four wells in the potato and vegetable mixture. Crack an egg into each well.

Cook Eggs:

- Cover the skillet and cook until the eggs are cooked to your liking. This may take about 5-7 minutes for eggs with runny yolks.

Add Black Beans and Tomatoes:
- Sprinkle cooked black beans and halved cherry tomatoes around the eggs. Allow them to heat through.

Melt Cheese:
- Sprinkle shredded cheddar cheese over the skillet. Cover and let it melt.

Garnish:
- Garnish the Southwest Potato and Egg Skillet with chopped fresh cilantro.

Serve:
- Serve the skillet hot with optional avocado slices and lime wedges on the side.

This Southwest-inspired skillet is a complete and satisfying breakfast or brunch dish. It's versatile, so feel free to customize it with your favorite toppings or adjust the spice level according to your taste preferences.

Potato and Chorizo Breakfast Tacos

Ingredients:

- 1 tablespoon olive oil
- 1 pound (about 450g) potatoes, diced into small cubes
- 1/2 pound (about 225g) chorizo sausage, casing removed
- 1 small onion, finely chopped
- 1 jalapeño, seeded and finely chopped (optional, for heat)
- 4 large eggs
- Salt and pepper, to taste
- 8 small corn or flour tortillas
- 1 cup shredded cheddar or Mexican blend cheese
- Fresh cilantro, chopped, for garnish
- Salsa, avocado slices, or hot sauce, for serving (optional)

Instructions:

Cook Potatoes:
- In a large skillet, heat olive oil over medium heat. Add diced potatoes and cook until they are golden brown and cooked through. This may take about 10-15 minutes.

Cook Chorizo and Vegetables:
- Push the potatoes to one side of the skillet. Add chorizo to the other side and cook, breaking it up with a spatula as it browns. Once the chorizo is cooked, mix it with the potatoes.
- Add chopped onion and jalapeño (if using) to the skillet. Sauté until the vegetables are softened.

Scramble Eggs:
- Push the potato-chorizo mixture to one side again. Crack the eggs into the skillet on the empty side. Scramble the eggs until they are cooked to your liking.

Combine and Season:
- Mix the scrambled eggs with the potato-chorizo mixture. Season with salt and pepper to taste. Ensure everything is well combined.

Warm Tortillas:
- Heat the tortillas in a dry skillet or warm them in the oven.

Assemble Tacos:
- Spoon the potato, chorizo, and egg mixture onto each tortilla.

Add Cheese and Garnish:
- Sprinkle shredded cheese over the filling. Garnish with chopped fresh cilantro.

Serve:
- Serve the Potato and Chorizo Breakfast Tacos hot, with salsa, avocado slices, or hot sauce on the side if desired.

These breakfast tacos are a delicious combination of savory flavors, and you can customize them with your favorite toppings. They make for a hearty and satisfying breakfast or brunch.

Side Dishes and Salads:

Warm Potato Salad with Mustard Vinaigrette

Ingredients:

- 2 pounds (about 900g) baby potatoes, washed and halved
- 2 tablespoons olive oil
- Salt and pepper, to taste
- 1 tablespoon Dijon mustard
- 2 tablespoons red wine vinegar
- 1/4 cup extra-virgin olive oil
- 2 cloves garlic, minced
- 2 tablespoons fresh parsley, chopped
- 2 green onions, thinly sliced

Instructions:

Boil Potatoes:
- Place the halved baby potatoes in a pot of cold, salted water. Bring to a boil and cook until the potatoes are fork-tender but not falling apart. This usually takes about 10-15 minutes.

Make Vinaigrette:
- While the potatoes are cooking, prepare the mustard vinaigrette. In a small bowl, whisk together Dijon mustard, red wine vinegar, extra-virgin olive oil, minced garlic, salt, and pepper. Adjust the seasoning to taste.

Drain and Toss Potatoes:
- Once the potatoes are cooked, drain them and transfer them to a large mixing bowl. While the potatoes are still warm, drizzle them with olive oil and toss to coat.

Add Vinaigrette:
- Pour the prepared mustard vinaigrette over the warm potatoes. Gently toss until the potatoes are well coated with the vinaigrette.

Garnish:
- Sprinkle chopped fresh parsley and thinly sliced green onions over the warm potato salad. Toss once more to distribute the herbs evenly.

Serve:
- Serve the Warm Potato Salad immediately as a side dish or a warm appetizer.

This warm potato salad is a delightful side dish that works well with a variety of main courses. It's a perfect addition to picnics, barbecues, or as a comforting side during cooler seasons.

Dill Pickle Potato Salad

Ingredients:

- 2 pounds (about 900g) baby potatoes, washed and halved
- 1 cup mayonnaise
- 1/4 cup Dijon mustard
- 1/4 cup chopped dill pickles
- 2 tablespoons pickle juice
- 2 tablespoons fresh dill, chopped
- 1/4 cup red onion, finely chopped
- Salt and pepper, to taste
- 2 hard-boiled eggs, chopped (optional, for garnish)

Instructions:

Boil Potatoes:
- Place the halved baby potatoes in a pot of cold, salted water. Bring to a boil and cook until the potatoes are fork-tender but not falling apart. This usually takes about 10-15 minutes.

Prepare Dressing:
- In a large mixing bowl, whisk together mayonnaise, Dijon mustard, chopped dill pickles, pickle juice, chopped fresh dill, and finely chopped red onion. Season with salt and pepper to taste.

Drain and Cool Potatoes:
- Once the potatoes are cooked, drain them and let them cool to room temperature.

Combine with Dressing:
- Add the cooled potatoes to the bowl with the dressing. Gently toss until the potatoes are well coated with the flavorful dressing.

Chill:
- Cover the bowl and refrigerate the Dill Pickle Potato Salad for at least 2 hours to allow the flavors to meld.

Garnish (Optional):
- Just before serving, garnish the potato salad with chopped hard-boiled eggs if desired.

Serve:

- Serve the Dill Pickle Potato Salad chilled as a side dish for picnics, barbecues, or alongside your favorite main courses.

This potato salad is a delightful combination of creamy, tangy, and dill-infused flavors.

It's a perfect dish for those who love the zesty taste of dill pickles.

Lemon Herb Roasted Potato Salad

Ingredients:

- 2 pounds (about 900g) baby potatoes, washed and halved
- 2 tablespoons olive oil
- Zest of 1 lemon
- Juice of 1 lemon
- 2 cloves garlic, minced
- 1 teaspoon Dijon mustard
- 1 tablespoon fresh thyme, chopped
- 1 tablespoon fresh rosemary, chopped
- Salt and pepper, to taste
- 1/4 cup fresh parsley, chopped
- 1/4 cup red onion, finely chopped
- 1/4 cup feta cheese, crumbled (optional)

Instructions:

Preheat Oven:
- Preheat your oven to 400°F (200°C).

Roast Potatoes:
- In a large mixing bowl, combine halved baby potatoes with olive oil, lemon zest, lemon juice, minced garlic, Dijon mustard, chopped thyme, chopped rosemary, salt, and pepper. Toss until the potatoes are evenly coated.
- Spread the potatoes in a single layer on a baking sheet lined with parchment paper. Roast in the preheated oven for about 25-30 minutes or until the potatoes are golden brown and crispy on the edges. Toss them halfway through for even cooking.

Prepare Dressing:
- While the potatoes are roasting, mix together fresh parsley, finely chopped red onion, and crumbled feta cheese (if using) in a small bowl.

Combine:
- Once the roasted potatoes are done, transfer them to a serving bowl. Add the prepared parsley, red onion, and feta mixture. Gently toss to combine.

Adjust Seasoning:
- Taste the potato salad and adjust the seasoning if needed with additional salt, pepper, or lemon juice.

Serve:
- Serve the Lemon Herb Roasted Potato Salad warm or at room temperature as a flavorful side dish.

This potato salad is a delightful combination of roasted potatoes with the bright flavors of lemon and a medley of fresh herbs. It's a perfect dish for spring and summer gatherings.

Sweet Potato and Black Bean Salad

Ingredients:

For the Salad:

- 2 large sweet potatoes, peeled and diced
- 1 can (15 ounces) black beans, drained and rinsed
- 1 cup corn kernels (fresh or frozen)
- 1 red bell pepper, diced
- 1/2 red onion, finely chopped
- 1/4 cup fresh cilantro, chopped
- Salt and pepper, to taste

For the Dressing:

- 3 tablespoons olive oil
- 2 tablespoons lime juice
- 1 teaspoon ground cumin
- 1 teaspoon chili powder
- Salt and pepper, to taste

Instructions:

Roast Sweet Potatoes:
- Preheat your oven to 400°F (200°C). Toss the diced sweet potatoes with a bit of olive oil, salt, and pepper. Spread them on a baking sheet and roast in the oven for about 20-25 minutes or until they are tender and lightly browned.

Prepare Black Beans and Corn:
- In a large bowl, combine the black beans, corn, diced red bell pepper, finely chopped red onion, and chopped cilantro.

Make Dressing:
- In a small bowl, whisk together olive oil, lime juice, ground cumin, chili powder, salt, and pepper.

Combine Ingredients:
- Once the sweet potatoes are roasted, add them to the bowl with the black bean mixture.

Add Dressing:

- Pour the dressing over the salad ingredients.

Toss and Season:
- Gently toss all the ingredients together until they are well coated with the dressing. Taste and adjust the seasoning if needed.

Chill (Optional):
- You can chill the Sweet Potato and Black Bean Salad in the refrigerator for about 30 minutes before serving if you prefer it cold.

Serve:
- Serve the salad as a side dish or a light main course. It's great on its own or paired with grilled chicken or fish.

This Sweet Potato and Black Bean Salad is not only delicious but also full of vibrant colors and textures. It makes a fantastic addition to picnics, barbecues, or as a healthy lunch option.

Caprese Potato Salad

Ingredients:

- 2 pounds (about 900g) baby potatoes, washed and halved
- 1 cup cherry tomatoes, halved
- 1 cup fresh mozzarella balls (bocconcini), halved
- 1/4 cup fresh basil leaves, torn
- 1/4 cup extra-virgin olive oil
- 2 tablespoons balsamic vinegar
- Salt and pepper, to taste
- 1 clove garlic, minced (optional)
- Balsamic glaze, for drizzling (optional)

Instructions:

Boil Potatoes:
- Place the halved baby potatoes in a pot of cold, salted water. Bring to a boil and cook until the potatoes are fork-tender but not falling apart. This usually takes about 10-15 minutes.

Prepare Dressing:
- In a small bowl, whisk together extra-virgin olive oil, balsamic vinegar, minced garlic (if using), salt, and pepper.

Drain and Cool Potatoes:
- Once the potatoes are cooked, drain them and let them cool to room temperature.

Combine Ingredients:
- In a large mixing bowl, combine the cooled potatoes with cherry tomatoes, fresh mozzarella balls, and torn basil leaves.

Add Dressing:
- Pour the prepared dressing over the potato mixture. Gently toss until the ingredients are well coated with the dressing.

Chill (Optional):
- You can chill the Caprese Potato Salad in the refrigerator for about 30 minutes before serving if you prefer it cold.

Drizzle with Balsamic Glaze (Optional):
- Just before serving, drizzle the salad with balsamic glaze for an extra burst of flavor.

Serve:
- Serve the Caprese Potato Salad as a refreshing side dish or a light main course. It's perfect for summer gatherings or as a tasty addition to your barbecue.

This potato salad combines the classic Caprese ingredients with tender potatoes for a delightful and satisfying dish. The balsamic glaze adds a touch of sweetness and acidity, enhancing the overall flavor.

Potato and Green Bean Salad

Ingredients:

- 1 1/2 pounds (about 680g) baby potatoes, halved or quartered if large
- 8 ounces (about 225g) fresh green beans, trimmed and cut into bite-sized pieces
- 1/4 cup red onion, finely chopped
- 2 tablespoons fresh parsley, chopped
- 2 tablespoons fresh dill, chopped

For the Dressing:

- 1/4 cup extra-virgin olive oil
- 2 tablespoons red wine vinegar
- 1 teaspoon Dijon mustard
- 1 clove garlic, minced
- Salt and pepper, to taste

Instructions:

Boil Potatoes:
- Place the halved or quartered baby potatoes in a pot of cold, salted water. Bring to a boil and cook until the potatoes are fork-tender but not falling apart. This usually takes about 10-15 minutes.

Blanch Green Beans:
- In the last 3-4 minutes of the potato cooking time, add the fresh green beans to the boiling water. Blanch them until they are bright green and crisp-tender. Drain the potatoes and green beans and let them cool to room temperature.

Prepare Dressing:
- In a small bowl, whisk together extra-virgin olive oil, red wine vinegar, Dijon mustard, minced garlic, salt, and pepper to create the dressing.

Combine Ingredients:
- In a large mixing bowl, combine the cooled potatoes, blanched green beans, finely chopped red onion, fresh parsley, and fresh dill.

Add Dressing:
- Pour the dressing over the potato and green bean mixture. Gently toss until everything is well coated with the dressing.

Chill (Optional):
- You can chill the Potato and Green Bean Salad in the refrigerator for about 30 minutes before serving if you prefer it cold.

Serve:
- Serve the salad as a side dish or a light main course. It pairs well with grilled chicken, fish, or as part of a summer spread.

This Potato and Green Bean Salad is a flavorful and nutritious option, showcasing the natural goodness of fresh vegetables. Enjoy!

Moroccan Spiced Roasted Potatoes

Ingredients:

- 2 pounds (about 900g) baby potatoes, washed and quartered
- 3 tablespoons olive oil
- 1 teaspoon ground cumin
- 1 teaspoon ground coriander
- 1 teaspoon ground paprika
- 1/2 teaspoon ground cinnamon
- 1/2 teaspoon ground turmeric
- 1/2 teaspoon cayenne pepper (adjust to taste for heat)
- Salt and pepper, to taste
- 2 cloves garlic, minced
- 1 tablespoon fresh cilantro, chopped (for garnish)
- 1 tablespoon fresh parsley, chopped (for garnish)
- Lemon wedges, for serving

Instructions:

Preheat Oven:
- Preheat your oven to 400°F (200°C).

Prepare Potatoes:
- In a large bowl, toss the quartered baby potatoes with olive oil until they are evenly coated.

Create Spice Mix:
- In a small bowl, mix together ground cumin, ground coriander, ground paprika, ground cinnamon, ground turmeric, cayenne pepper, salt, and pepper.

Coat Potatoes with Spice Mix:
- Sprinkle the spice mix over the potatoes and toss them until they are well coated with the spices.

Roast Potatoes:
- Spread the seasoned potatoes in a single layer on a baking sheet lined with parchment paper. Roast in the preheated oven for about 30-35 minutes or until the potatoes are golden brown and crispy on the edges. Flip them halfway through for even cooking.

Add Garlic:

- In the last 5 minutes of roasting, add minced garlic to the potatoes and toss to combine. Roast until the garlic is fragrant and the potatoes are fully cooked.

Garnish:
- Remove the roasted potatoes from the oven. Garnish with fresh chopped cilantro and parsley.

Serve:
- Serve the Moroccan Spiced Roasted Potatoes warm, accompanied by lemon wedges for squeezing over the top.

These Moroccan-spiced potatoes are a delicious and exotic side dish that pairs well with a variety of main courses. The combination of warm spices adds depth and flavor to the humble potato.

Roasted Sweet Potato and Chickpea Salad

Ingredients:

For the Roasted Sweet Potatoes and Chickpeas:

- 2 large sweet potatoes, peeled and diced
- 1 can (15 ounces) chickpeas, drained and rinsed
- 2 tablespoons olive oil
- 1 teaspoon ground cumin
- 1 teaspoon smoked paprika
- 1/2 teaspoon garlic powder
- Salt and pepper, to taste

For the Salad:

- 4 cups mixed salad greens (such as spinach or arugula)
- 1 cup cherry tomatoes, halved
- 1 cucumber, diced
- 1/4 cup red onion, thinly sliced

For the Dressing:

- 3 tablespoons olive oil
- 2 tablespoons balsamic vinegar
- 1 tablespoon maple syrup or honey
- Salt and pepper, to taste

Instructions:

Preheat Oven:
- Preheat your oven to 400°F (200°C).

Prepare Roasted Sweet Potatoes and Chickpeas:
- In a large bowl, toss the diced sweet potatoes and chickpeas with olive oil, ground cumin, smoked paprika, garlic powder, salt, and pepper until well coated.
- Spread the sweet potatoes and chickpeas on a baking sheet in a single layer. Roast in the preheated oven for about 25-30 minutes or until the sweet potatoes are tender and the chickpeas are crispy. Toss them halfway through for even cooking.

Make Dressing:
- In a small bowl, whisk together olive oil, balsamic vinegar, maple syrup or honey, salt, and pepper to create the dressing.

Assemble Salad:
- In a large serving bowl, combine the mixed salad greens, halved cherry tomatoes, diced cucumber, and thinly sliced red onion.
- Add the roasted sweet potatoes and chickpeas to the salad.

Drizzle with Dressing:
- Drizzle the dressing over the salad ingredients.

Toss and Serve:
- Gently toss the salad until all the ingredients are well coated with the dressing.

Serve:
- Serve the Roasted Sweet Potato and Chickpea Salad immediately, either as a side dish or a light main course.

This salad is not only delicious but also packed with nutrients and textures, making it a satisfying and healthy meal option. Enjoy!

Creamy Dijon Potato Salad

Ingredients:

- 2 pounds (about 900g) baby potatoes, washed and halved
- 1/2 cup mayonnaise
- 3 tablespoons Dijon mustard
- 2 tablespoons whole-grain mustard
- 2 tablespoons red wine vinegar
- 1/4 cup celery, finely chopped
- 1/4 cup red onion, finely chopped
- 2 tablespoons fresh chives, chopped
- Salt and pepper, to taste
- 2 hard-boiled eggs, chopped (optional, for garnish)

Instructions:

Boil Potatoes:
- Place the halved baby potatoes in a pot of cold, salted water. Bring to a boil and cook until the potatoes are fork-tender but not falling apart. This usually takes about 10-15 minutes.

Prepare Dressing:
- In a bowl, whisk together mayonnaise, Dijon mustard, whole-grain mustard, red wine vinegar, chopped celery, chopped red onion, chopped fresh chives, salt, and pepper.

Drain and Cool Potatoes:
- Once the potatoes are cooked, drain them and let them cool to room temperature.

Combine Ingredients:
- In a large mixing bowl, combine the cooled potatoes with the prepared creamy Dijon dressing. Gently toss until the potatoes are well coated.

Chill (Optional):
- You can chill the Creamy Dijon Potato Salad in the refrigerator for about 30 minutes before serving if you prefer it cold.

Garnish (Optional):
- Just before serving, garnish the potato salad with chopped hard-boiled eggs if desired.

Serve:

- Serve the Creamy Dijon Potato Salad as a flavorful side dish for picnics, barbecues, or alongside your favorite main courses.

This potato salad is a delightful combination of creamy and tangy flavors, and the addition of Dijon mustard gives it a unique and zesty kick.

Roasted Red Pepper and Potato Gratin

Ingredients:

- 3 large red bell peppers, roasted, peeled, and sliced
- 2 pounds (about 900g) potatoes, peeled and thinly sliced
- 1 onion, thinly sliced
- 2 cloves garlic, minced
- 1 cup grated Gruyère or Swiss cheese
- 1 cup heavy cream
- 1/2 cup chicken or vegetable broth
- 2 tablespoons unsalted butter
- 2 tablespoons all-purpose flour
- 1 teaspoon dried thyme
- Salt and pepper, to taste
- Fresh parsley, chopped, for garnish

Instructions:

Roast Red Peppers:
- Preheat your oven's broiler. Place the red bell peppers on a baking sheet and broil, turning occasionally, until the skin is charred and blistered. Transfer the roasted peppers to a bowl, cover with plastic wrap, and let them steam for about 10 minutes. Peel the skins, remove the seeds, and slice the peppers into strips.

Preheat Oven:
- Preheat your oven to 375°F (190°C).

Prepare Potatoes and Onions:
- In a large bowl, toss the thinly sliced potatoes, sliced onions, and minced garlic together.

Make Cheese Sauce:
- In a saucepan over medium heat, melt the butter. Stir in the flour and cook for 1-2 minutes until it forms a smooth paste. Gradually whisk in the heavy cream and chicken or vegetable broth. Continue whisking until the mixture thickens.
- Remove the saucepan from heat and stir in the grated cheese until it's melted and the sauce is smooth. Season with salt, pepper, and dried thyme.

Assemble Gratin:

- Grease a baking dish. Arrange a layer of potato and onion mixture at the bottom of the dish. Top with a layer of roasted red pepper strips. Pour some of the cheese sauce over the layers. Repeat the process until all ingredients are used, finishing with a layer of cheese sauce on top.

Bake:
- Cover the baking dish with foil and bake in the preheated oven for about 45-50 minutes or until the potatoes are tender.

Broil (Optional):
- If you'd like a golden crust on top, uncover the dish and broil for an additional 3-5 minutes until the top is bubbly and golden.

Garnish and Serve:
- Garnish the Roasted Red Pepper and Potato Gratin with fresh chopped parsley and serve hot.

This gratin is a rich and flavorful side dish that pairs well with roasted or grilled meats. Enjoy!

Creative Potato Recipes:

Truffle Parmesan Potato Stacks

Ingredients:

- 4 large potatoes, peeled and thinly sliced
- 1/2 cup grated Parmesan cheese
- 1/4 cup truffle-infused olive oil
- 2 cloves garlic, minced
- 1 teaspoon fresh thyme leaves
- Salt and pepper, to taste
- Chopped fresh parsley, for garnish (optional)

Instructions:

Preheat Oven:
- Preheat your oven to 375°F (190°C).

Prepare Potatoes:
- Peel the potatoes and thinly slice them. A mandoline slicer can be helpful for achieving uniform slices.

Prepare Truffle Parmesan Mixture:
- In a bowl, combine grated Parmesan cheese, truffle-infused olive oil, minced garlic, fresh thyme leaves, salt, and pepper. Mix well to create the truffle Parmesan mixture.

Coat Potato Slices:
- Lightly coat each potato slice with the truffle Parmesan mixture, ensuring each slice is well coated.

Assemble Stacks:
- Arrange the coated potato slices vertically in a greased muffin tin or a baking dish. Stack them to form individual stacks.

Bake:
- Bake in the preheated oven for about 45-50 minutes or until the edges are golden brown, and the potatoes are cooked through. You can cover the stacks with foil for the first 30 minutes to prevent excessive browning.

Cool and Garnish:
- Allow the Truffle Parmesan Potato Stacks to cool slightly before carefully removing them from the muffin tin or baking dish. Garnish with chopped fresh parsley if desired.

Serve:
- Serve the potato stacks warm as a sophisticated and flavorful side dish.

These Truffle Parmesan Potato Stacks are a perfect choice for special occasions or when you want to elevate your dinner with a touch of luxury. The truffle-infused oil and Parmesan add a rich and earthy flavor to the crispy potato layers.

Loaded Potato Pierogi

Ingredients:

For the Dough:

- 2 cups all-purpose flour
- 1/2 teaspoon salt
- 1 large egg
- 1/2 cup sour cream
- 1/4 cup unsalted butter, melted

For the Potato Filling:

- 4 large potatoes, peeled and diced
- 1 cup shredded cheddar cheese
- 1/2 cup sour cream
- 4 slices bacon, cooked and crumbled
- 2 green onions, thinly sliced
- Salt and pepper, to taste

For Topping:

- 1/2 cup sour cream
- 2 tablespoons chopped chives or green onions
- Crumbled bacon (optional)

Instructions:

Prepare the Dough:
- In a large bowl, combine the flour and salt. In a separate bowl, whisk together the egg, sour cream, and melted butter. Gradually add the wet ingredients to the dry ingredients, stirring until a dough forms. Knead the dough on a floured surface until smooth. Cover and let it rest for 30 minutes.

Make the Potato Filling:

- Boil the diced potatoes until tender. Drain and mash the potatoes. Mix in shredded cheddar cheese, sour cream, crumbled bacon, sliced green onions, salt, and pepper. Adjust the seasoning to taste.

Roll Out the Dough:
- Roll out the dough on a floured surface to about 1/8-inch thickness. Use a round cookie cutter or a glass to cut out circles from the dough.

Fill the Dough:
- Place a small spoonful of the potato filling in the center of each dough circle. Fold the dough in half, sealing the edges to form a crescent shape. You can use a fork to crimp the edges for a decorative touch.

Cook the Pierogi:
- Bring a large pot of salted water to a boil. Cook the pierogi in batches for about 3-4 minutes, or until they float to the surface. Remove them with a slotted spoon and transfer to a plate.

Optional: Sauté the Pierogi:
- For added flavor, you can sauté the boiled pierogi in butter until they are golden brown on each side.

Serve:
- Mix sour cream and chopped chives or green onions for a dipping sauce. Serve the Loaded Potato Pierogi hot, drizzled with the sour cream mixture and additional crumbled bacon if desired.

These Loaded Potato Pierogi are a delicious and comforting dish that combines the classic flavors of loaded baked potatoes with the delightful texture of pierogi. Enjoy!

Pesto Potato Pizzas

Ingredients:

For the Potato Crust:

- 4 medium-sized potatoes, peeled and grated
- 1 egg
- 1/4 cup all-purpose flour
- Salt and pepper, to taste
- Olive oil, for brushing

For the Pesto:

- 2 cups fresh basil leaves
- 1/2 cup grated Parmesan cheese
- 1/2 cup pine nuts or walnuts
- 2 cloves garlic, minced
- 1/2 cup extra-virgin olive oil
- Salt and pepper, to taste

Toppings:

- Cherry tomatoes, sliced
- Mozzarella cheese, shredded
- Fresh basil leaves, for garnish

Instructions:

Preheat Oven:
- Preheat your oven to 400°F (200°C).

Make the Potato Crust:
- Place the grated potatoes in a clean kitchen towel and squeeze out excess moisture. In a bowl, combine the grated potatoes, egg, flour, salt, and pepper. Mix until well combined.
- Divide the potato mixture into portions and shape them into small pizza crusts on a baking sheet lined with parchment paper.
- Brush the potato crusts with olive oil and bake in the preheated oven for about 20-25 minutes or until the edges are golden and the crusts are cooked through.

Prepare the Pesto:
- In a food processor, combine fresh basil, grated Parmesan cheese, pine nuts or walnuts, minced garlic, salt, and pepper. Pulse until finely chopped.
- With the food processor running, slowly pour in the olive oil until the pesto reaches your desired consistency. Adjust salt and pepper to taste.

Assemble the Pesto Potato Pizzas:
- Once the potato crusts are cooked, spread a layer of pesto over each crust.
- Top with sliced cherry tomatoes and shredded mozzarella cheese.

Bake Again:
- Return the pizzas to the oven and bake for an additional 10-12 minutes, or until the cheese is melted and bubbly.

Garnish and Serve:
- Remove the Pesto Potato Pizzas from the oven. Garnish with fresh basil leaves and serve hot.

These Pesto Potato Pizzas offer a gluten-free and unique twist to traditional pizza, combining the earthy flavors of potatoes with the freshness of basil pesto. Enjoy these delightful mini pizzas as a creative appetizer or a flavorful snack.

Potato and Leek Soup

Ingredients:

- 3 leeks, cleaned and sliced (white and light green parts only)
- 3 large potatoes, peeled and diced
- 1 onion, chopped
- 2 cloves garlic, minced
- 4 cups vegetable or chicken broth
- 1 cup milk or heavy cream (for a creamier version)
- 2 tablespoons butter or olive oil
- Salt and pepper, to taste
- Fresh chives or parsley, chopped (for garnish, optional)

Instructions:

Prepare Leeks:
- Clean the leeks thoroughly to remove any dirt. Slice them into thin rounds, using only the white and light green parts.

Sauté Vegetables:
- In a large pot, melt the butter or heat olive oil over medium heat. Add chopped onions, sliced leeks, and minced garlic. Sauté until the vegetables are softened, but not browned.

Add Potatoes:
- Add the diced potatoes to the pot. Stir to combine with the sautéed vegetables.

Pour in Broth:
- Pour in the vegetable or chicken broth, ensuring that the potatoes are mostly covered. Bring the mixture to a boil, then reduce the heat to simmer. Cook until the potatoes are tender, usually around 15-20 minutes.

Blend (Optional):
- For a smoother consistency, you can use an immersion blender to blend the soup to your desired smoothness. Alternatively, transfer a portion of the soup to a blender and blend until smooth, then return it to the pot.

Add Milk or Cream:
- Stir in the milk or heavy cream to add creaminess to the soup. Adjust the amount based on your preference.

Season:

- Season the soup with salt and pepper to taste. Adjust the seasoning as needed.

Simmer:
- Allow the soup to simmer for an additional 5-10 minutes to let the flavors meld together.

Garnish and Serve:
- Ladle the Potato and Leek Soup into bowls. Garnish with chopped fresh chives or parsley if desired.

Enjoy this hearty and flavorful Potato and Leek Soup as a comforting meal, especially during colder seasons. Serve it with crusty bread for a complete and satisfying experience.

Baked Potato Pizza with Bacon and Ranch

Ingredients:

For the Pizza Dough:

- 1 pound pizza dough (store-bought or homemade)
- Cornmeal or flour, for dusting

For the Toppings:

- 2 large potatoes, thinly sliced
- Olive oil
- Salt and pepper, to taste
- 1 cup shredded cheddar cheese
- 1 cup shredded mozzarella cheese
- 6 slices bacon, cooked and crumbled
- Green onions, chopped, for garnish
- Ranch dressing, for drizzling

Instructions:

Preheat Oven:
- Preheat your oven according to the pizza dough package instructions or recipe guidelines.

Prepare Potatoes:
- Thinly slice the potatoes (use a mandoline slicer for even slices). Toss the potato slices with olive oil, salt, and pepper.

Cook Potatoes:
- In a skillet over medium heat, cook the seasoned potato slices until they are slightly tender and golden brown on the edges. Set aside.

Roll Out Pizza Dough:
- On a floured surface or cornmeal-dusted pizza peel, roll out the pizza dough to your desired thickness.

Assemble Pizza:

- Transfer the rolled-out dough to a pizza stone or a baking sheet. Brush the dough with olive oil. Sprinkle a layer of shredded cheddar and mozzarella cheese over the dough.
- Arrange the cooked potato slices evenly over the cheese. Sprinkle the crumbled bacon on top.

Bake:
- Bake the pizza in the preheated oven according to the pizza dough instructions or until the crust is golden and the cheese is melted and bubbly.

Garnish and Serve:
- Once out of the oven, garnish the Baked Potato Pizza with chopped green onions and drizzle with ranch dressing.

Slice and Enjoy:
- Slice the pizza and serve it hot. Enjoy the delicious combination of flavors reminiscent of a loaded baked potato.

This Baked Potato Pizza with Bacon and Ranch is a delightful treat that combines the goodness of a classic baked potato with the convenience of a pizza. It's perfect for a cozy night in or a fun family dinner.

Miso Glazed Sweet Potatoes

Ingredients:

- 2 large sweet potatoes, peeled and cut into wedges or cubes
- 2 tablespoons white or red miso paste
- 2 tablespoons maple syrup or honey
- 1 tablespoon soy sauce or tamari (for a gluten-free option)
- 1 tablespoon rice vinegar
- 1 tablespoon sesame oil
- 1 teaspoon grated fresh ginger
- 2 cloves garlic, minced
- Sesame seeds and chopped green onions for garnish (optional)

Instructions:

Preheat Oven:
- Preheat your oven to 400°F (200°C).

Prepare Sweet Potatoes:
- Peel the sweet potatoes and cut them into wedges or cubes, ensuring they are of similar size for even cooking.

Make Miso Glaze:
- In a bowl, whisk together miso paste, maple syrup or honey, soy sauce or tamari, rice vinegar, sesame oil, grated ginger, and minced garlic until well combined.

Coat Sweet Potatoes:
- Place the sweet potato wedges or cubes in a large bowl. Pour the miso glaze over the sweet potatoes and toss until they are evenly coated.

Roast:
- Spread the coated sweet potatoes in a single layer on a baking sheet lined with parchment paper. Roast in the preheated oven for 25-30 minutes or until the sweet potatoes are tender and caramelized, turning them halfway through for even cooking.

Garnish (Optional):
- If desired, garnish the Miso Glazed Sweet Potatoes with sesame seeds and chopped green onions.

Serve:
- Serve the sweet potatoes hot as a flavorful side dish.

This Miso Glazed Sweet Potatoes recipe offers a balance of sweetness and umami, creating a delicious and unique twist on roasted sweet potatoes. It's a perfect side dish for various meals, and the miso glaze adds a depth of flavor that makes it truly special.

Potato and Mushroom Tacos

Ingredients:

- 2 large sweet potatoes, peeled and cut into wedges or cubes
- 2 tablespoons white or red miso paste
- 2 tablespoons maple syrup or honey
- 1 tablespoon soy sauce or tamari (for a gluten-free option)
- 1 tablespoon rice vinegar
- 1 tablespoon sesame oil
- 1 teaspoon grated fresh ginger
- 2 cloves garlic, minced
- Sesame seeds and chopped green onions for garnish (optional)

Instructions:

Preheat Oven:
- Preheat your oven to 400°F (200°C).

Prepare Sweet Potatoes:
- Peel the sweet potatoes and cut them into wedges or cubes, ensuring they are of similar size for even cooking.

Make Miso Glaze:
- In a bowl, whisk together miso paste, maple syrup or honey, soy sauce or tamari, rice vinegar, sesame oil, grated ginger, and minced garlic until well combined.

Coat Sweet Potatoes:
- Place the sweet potato wedges or cubes in a large bowl. Pour the miso glaze over the sweet potatoes and toss until they are evenly coated.

Roast:
- Spread the coated sweet potatoes in a single layer on a baking sheet lined with parchment paper. Roast in the preheated oven for 25-30 minutes or until the sweet potatoes are tender and caramelized, turning them halfway through for even cooking.

Garnish (Optional):
- If desired, garnish the Miso Glazed Sweet Potatoes with sesame seeds and chopped green onions.

Serve:
- Serve the sweet potatoes hot as a flavorful side dish.

This Miso Glazed Sweet Potatoes recipe offers a balance of sweetness and umami, creating a delicious and unique twist on roasted sweet potatoes. It's a perfect side dish for various meals, and the miso glaze adds a depth of flavor that makes it truly special.

Greek Feta and Olive Stuffed Sweet Potatoes

Ingredients:

- 4 medium-sized sweet potatoes
- 1 cup crumbled feta cheese
- 1/2 cup Kalamata olives, pitted and chopped
- 1/4 cup red onion, finely chopped
- 2 tablespoons fresh parsley, chopped
- 1 tablespoon extra-virgin olive oil
- 1 teaspoon dried oregano
- Salt and pepper, to taste
- Lemon wedges, for serving

Instructions:

Preheat Oven:
- Preheat your oven to 400°F (200°C).

Roast Sweet Potatoes:
- Wash the sweet potatoes and prick them with a fork. Place them on a baking sheet and bake in the preheated oven for about 45-60 minutes or until they are tender. The baking time may vary depending on the size of the sweet potatoes.

Prepare Filling:
- While the sweet potatoes are baking, prepare the filling. In a bowl, combine crumbled feta cheese, chopped Kalamata olives, finely chopped red onion, chopped fresh parsley, extra-virgin olive oil, dried oregano, salt, and pepper. Mix well.

Slice Sweet Potatoes:
- Once the sweet potatoes are cooked, let them cool slightly. Slice each sweet potato in half lengthwise without cutting all the way through.

Fluff and Stuff:
- Gently fluff the insides of the sweet potatoes with a fork. Spoon the feta and olive filling into the center of each sweet potato, distributing it evenly among them.

Bake Again:

- Place the stuffed sweet potatoes back in the oven for an additional 10-15 minutes, or until the filling is heated through, and the sweet potatoes are slightly crispy on the edges.

Serve:
- Remove the Greek Feta and Olive Stuffed Sweet Potatoes from the oven. Serve them warm with lemon wedges on the side.

This dish offers a delightful combination of sweet, salty, and savory flavors, making it a satisfying and delicious option for a wholesome meal. Enjoy!

Cajun Spiced Potato Wedge Nachos

Ingredients:

For the Potato Wedges:

- 4 large russet potatoes, washed and cut into wedges
- 2 tablespoons olive oil
- 1 tablespoon Cajun seasoning
- 1 teaspoon garlic powder
- 1 teaspoon onion powder
- Salt and pepper, to taste

For the Nacho Toppings:

- 1 cup shredded cheddar cheese
- 1 cup cooked and shredded chicken (optional)
- 1/2 cup diced tomatoes
- 1/4 cup sliced green onions
- 1/4 cup sliced black olives
- Sour cream, guacamole, and salsa for serving

Instructions:

Preheat Oven:
- Preheat your oven to 425°F (220°C).

Prepare Potato Wedges:
- In a large bowl, toss the potato wedges with olive oil, Cajun seasoning, garlic powder, onion powder, salt, and pepper until the wedges are evenly coated.

Bake Potato Wedges:
- Spread the seasoned potato wedges in a single layer on a baking sheet lined with parchment paper. Bake in the preheated oven for about 30-35 minutes or until the wedges are golden brown and crispy, flipping them halfway through for even cooking.

Assemble Nachos:
- Once the potato wedges are cooked, arrange them on a serving platter or a large plate. Sprinkle shredded cheddar cheese over the wedges.
- If using, distribute the cooked and shredded chicken over the cheese.

- Add diced tomatoes, sliced green onions, and sliced black olives as desired.

Broil (Optional):
- If you'd like the cheese to melt and become bubbly, you can place the nachos under the broiler for 1-2 minutes, keeping a close eye to prevent burning.

Serve:
- Remove the Cajun Spiced Potato Wedge Nachos from the oven. Serve them hot with sides of sour cream, guacamole, and salsa.

These nachos offer a spicy Cajun kick with the crispy texture of seasoned potato wedges. Customize the toppings to your liking, and enjoy this unique and delicious take on classic nachos.

Potato and Corn Chowder

Ingredients:

- 4 cups potatoes, peeled and diced
- 1 cup onion, finely chopped
- 1 cup celery, chopped
- 1 cup carrots, diced
- 2 cups corn kernels (fresh, frozen, or canned)
- 4 cups vegetable or chicken broth
- 2 cups milk
- 1/4 cup all-purpose flour
- 4 tablespoons butter
- 1 teaspoon dried thyme
- 1/2 teaspoon smoked paprika
- Salt and pepper, to taste
- Fresh parsley, chopped (for garnish, optional)

Instructions:

Prepare Vegetables:
- Peel and dice the potatoes, finely chop the onion, chop the celery, and dice the carrots.

Cook Vegetables:
- In a large pot, melt butter over medium heat. Add onions, celery, and carrots. Sauté until the vegetables are softened.

Add Flour:
- Sprinkle the flour over the sautéed vegetables and stir well to coat. Cook for 2-3 minutes to remove the raw taste of the flour.

Pour in Broth:
- Gradually pour in the vegetable or chicken broth, stirring continuously to avoid lumps. Bring the mixture to a simmer.

Add Potatoes and Corn:
- Add diced potatoes and corn kernels to the pot. Simmer until the potatoes are tender, about 15-20 minutes.

Season:
- Stir in dried thyme, smoked paprika, salt, and pepper. Adjust the seasoning to taste.

Add Milk:
- Pour in the milk, stirring constantly. Continue to simmer for an additional 5-10 minutes until the chowder thickens.

Check Consistency:
- If the chowder is too thick, you can add more milk or broth to reach your desired consistency.

Serve:
- Ladle the Potato and Corn Chowder into bowls. Garnish with chopped fresh parsley if desired.

Enjoy this warm and creamy Potato and Corn Chowder as a comforting meal, especially on chilly days. Serve it with crusty bread or crackers for a complete and satisfying experience.